# THE BAND'S GUIDE TO GETTING A RECORD DEAL

## 2ND EDITION

Printed in the United Kingdom by MPG Books Ltd, Bodmin

Published by Sanctuary Publishing Limited, Sanctuary House, 45–53 Sinclair Road,
London W14 0NS, United Kingdom

www.sanctuarypublishing.com

Distributed in the US by Publishers Group West

ISBN: 1-86074-629-2

# THE
# BAND'S
# GUIDE TO
# GETTING A
# RECORD
# DEAL

**2ND EDITION**

Will Ashurst

Sanctuary

# ACKNOWLEDGMENTS

All of the following people have enriched the time I have spent in the music business, and to each of them I owe a debt of gratitude (and in some cases, actual cash): Ian Sands, Chris Preston, Jonnie Stockdale, Ralph Atherton, Graham Walsh, Martin J Haxby, Gareth Hopkins, Charles Law, Steve Cooke, Dave King, Sarah Best, Debrina Lloyd-Davies, Simon Wilson, Davy Simpson, Steve Tannett, Miles Copeland, Duncan Smith, Ollie Smith, Martin Jackson, Carol Decker, Andy Taylor, Rod Smallwood, Aky Najeeb, Andrea Levy, Andy Graham, Mike Hopkins, Michelle Margherita and Andrew Campbell, plus an all-enveloping 'thank you' to anyone who has ever done me a favour.

As CJ used to say to Reggie Perrin, 'I didn't get where I am today…' without the following people, to all of whom I owe a lot more than I can ever repay: my family – Mum, Dad, Kate and Jez; Penny Mallinson, Lucy Osborne, Charlie Walker and Martin R Smith.

# CONTENTS

## INTRODUCTION

## CHAPTERS

# APPENDICES

# INTRODUCTION

## The Music Industry Today

The British music industry today is a respected creative industry which has enormous cultural influence and significance worldwide.

During the 1960s and 1970s, the music business was seen as the home of mavericks, sharks, shady dealers and wild characters. To the Establishment and, perhaps more significantly, to the City, the music business was regarded as more than slightly tawdry, a fickle marketplace where only true entrepreneurs would invest their time and money.

Today, music-industry figures have the ability to influence government policy, not just in its relationships with the creative industries but on a wider scale of issues ranging from drugs to youth employment. The music industry is a massive export earner for Britain, comparable in size to the steel industry, and has a direct and immediate impact on the worldwide perception of British culture.

For a country with a total population of around 60 million, our music has more influence on a worldwide scale than perhaps any other of our industries, and certainly any other aspect of our popular culture. The UK accounts for 7% of global annual music sales of £25 billion and, more significantly, almost 20% of all music sales across the world are made by artists of UK origin. Artists such as In recent years, Dido, Coldplay, Joss Stone and Robbie Williams have kept the UK music business's profile high throughout the world.

It is estimated that there are more than 1,000 record companies in the UK (and, within them, hundreds more so-called 'labels' or imprints), ranging from bedsit operations releasing albums of birdsong to huge players with a massively diverse A&R policy, such as EMI, who compete on the world stage with the other 'majors': Sony/BMG, Universal and Warner Music.

The UK remains the home to the culture of the independent label, the numbers of which burgeoned at the same time as the punk boom of the mid 1970s.

Prior to punk, the UK music business was effectively in the control of the majors, which many would argue led to a creative stagnation in the development of new talent. Punk's DIY ideology demystified the industry and, more importantly, attracted some of the most visionary people working in the business today into their first jobs. In terms of the media, punk also led to a complete rethink within the music press, radio and television, breaking down yet more barriers to the development of new artists.

One of the great advantages the UK music business has over the US industry is the sheer compactness of the UK as a marketplace, in relation to the worldwide influence its industry wields. Britain's small size makes distribution, marketing and promotion relatively easy, and supports effective touring by artists. Even the smaller towns in the UK have a healthy live music scene. Radio, television, print media and online media, although much larger in terms of numbers of outlets than they were ten years ago, are still relatively accessible and affordable for marketing artists. Despite the contrary impression sometimes arising, UK consumers spend a high proportion of their income on leisure and recreational pursuits, including the purchase of music products. For these reasons, there may be no better place in the world to get a record or publishing deal, or to find rewarding and challenging work in the music industry.

Yet the industry faces problems, not least its relationship with new technology and the Internet. Now, after the format wars of the '80s and '90s, when CD established its supremacy over first vinyl and then cassette, and latterly MiniDisc beat DCC, the record companies need to look forward to reselling huge amounts of catalogue recordings digitally to keep their coffers full. The global industry has been incredibly slow in getting to grips with digital distribution, and many would suggest that this has meant the industry has almost signed its own death warrant, at least in terms of leadership in distribution itself.

Breaking new artists and at the same time cutting costs are paramount. The threat of the Internet is that it potentially undermines the basic foundations upon which record companies and record retailers are built. In effect, digital distribution of music is a double-edged sword, on the one hand offering instantaneous access to content at reasonable prices whilst on the other hand threatening traditional distribution and retail models. In coming to terms with the new world order, the majors have only recently begun to offer online sales of their existing product in any cohesive way. All record companies now offer a choice of recordings for purchase via their websites, and with the advent of OD2, Napster, iTunes and countless others the long-predicted 'Death Of The Single' looks imminent, and the traditional album format is certainly being seriously questioned for the first time. Sales of digital music players now account for one in three of all sales of personal stereos.

A more familiar problem is piracy, especially given the increasing cheapness of manufacturing technology and the lack of effective anti-piracy legislation in a significant number of countries. For an industry based firmly on the ownership and exploitation of intellectual property rights, the Internet and piracy as a joint threat could lead to a nightmare scenario. Only in recent years has the industry been mobilising to tackle web piracy by working with technology companies on encryption and delivery systems. With the advent of cheap CDRs and the explosion in home-computer ownership, the perceived value of artists and recordings is lessening. Surveys provide conflicting evidence of the effect of file sharing, with a certain amount of credible evidence emerging that the greater the amount of apparent file sharing relating to a particular artist, then the greater the increase in legitimate sales of their CDs at retail and via legitimate downloads. Many in the industry, whilst understanding the frustrations that have led to industry bodies suing file sharers, question the long-term wisdom of any industry criminalising its consumers.

A long-term problem for artists is the reduction in the sheer number of record companies that operate on a meaningful level. Increasingly, independent labels that show signs of developing interesting (ie profitable) artists are bought out by the majors, either purchased outright or invested into by way of distribution and licensing arrangements.

The danger here is that massive conglomerates inevitably try to cut costs by streamlining staff and centralising administration, which can lead to less adventurous A&R policies and an over-reliance on catalogue sales. None of this is good news for new acts.

Artists such as David Bowie have already issued bonds secured on their future earnings directly to investors, and many other major artists who are out of contract have decided to embrace the digital era, remain free of long-term agreements and issue their own product at up to seven times the margin they would otherwise make if they signed to another label. Ultimately, the ugly truth is that a fully packaged compact disc, complete with jewel case and booklet, costs less than 30p to make, plus whatever publishing payments are due – and even these are unlikely to make the total cost much over £1. One recent example of a major artist having huge success by going it alone and releasing their own product is Simply Red, who are one of hundreds of established artists who are sustaining a very successful career outside the model of a traditional major record deal.

It is an unfortunate fact that, in recent years, TV shows such as PopStars, Pop Idol and The X Factor have produced an extremely distorted impression in many people's minds as to how the real music industry works. It would not be entirely surprising, given the antics of the judges and contestants on these shows, if potential investors in the industry had been put off for life. Apart from selecting one or two artists who have gone on to achieve significant album sales, none of these shows have produced much in the way of artists with any long-term future. Of course, there has always been pop, and there have always been 'manufactured' artists, but to reveal the sometimes hideous inner workings of that side of the industry on primetime TV is seen by many as extremely damaging.

Artists have a potentially longer lifespan than ever, which causes as many problems as it solves. Increasingly, artists who have had huge success in the past are being dropped by major labels and finding homes at smaller, less established companies who might otherwise invest in new talent. It's an example of the law of diminishing returns, as many such artists still require or demand huge investment in areas such as recording costs and videos, making the consequences of sales failure all the more serious. The concept of an artist 'retiring' seems to have become a thing of the past, and the industry is top-heavy with former stars who are unwilling to call it a day while there is still a small demand for their work. On a practical level, the sheer number of rack spaces in record shops needs to grow constantly to cope with the volume of product being produced. Industry executives – who, after all, are the ones to blame – say it time and time again: there is simply too much product being released.

In recent years, too, we have seen the unexpected failure of major artists who have commanded huge advances to deliver albums generating the necessary high sales to recoup their record company's investment. If a company such as Universal had a year with less than successful albums from artists such as U2, Elton John or Bon Jovi, the consequences for the company worldwide would affect even the smallest acts on the smallest of its labels. In addition, it is less certain than ever that an artist will be able to repeat anywhere near the sales levels of a hugely successful debut album, when its record company's expectations have never been higher.

# SALES BY GENRE 2003

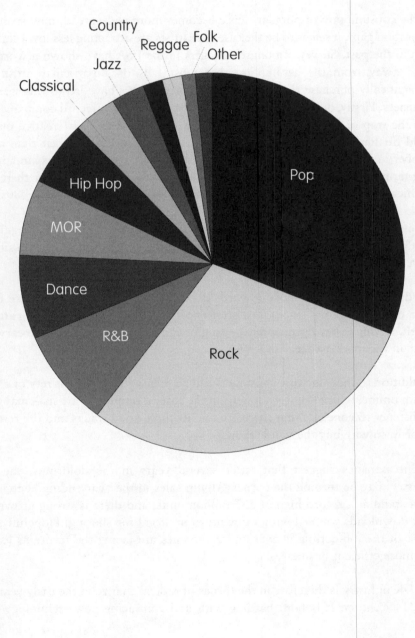

Music tastes are becoming more regionalised, with a dwindling number of truly international sales performers as consumers worldwide return to favouring artists who perform in their native language. This trend has been assisted by the decentralisation of media such as MTV, the explosion in the number of cable and satellite channels, and restrictions in certain territories on the amount of non-domestic music that is permitted to be broadcast and sold.

As the consumption of popular music becomes more widespread, now spanning generation gaps, it seems to be the case that artists are attracting less loyal support than in the past. Surveys amongst teenagers in the USA have shown a worrying trend away from the assumption that most fans of a particular artist will automatically purchase their next album. Three factors have led to this seeming fickleness. Firstly, during the mid to late 1980s, particularly, record companies fell into the trap of believing that almost any artist, whatever their creative merits, could be marketed to success. This led to the emergence of a larger than usual number of highly stylised and ephemeral artists with a short career span and no long-term artistic potential. Few industry executives would argue that there is a significant lack of long-term catalogue artists whose career began in the '80s.

Secondly, established artists fell out of the pattern of releasing albums regularly, with gaps of several years between product, during which their audiences simply moved on.

Thirdly, the worldwide move towards dance music, which gathered pace from 1988 onwards but has since tailed off, has produced few artists of lasting artistic worth, relying instead principally on singles and compilation albums to carve its niche in the marketplace.

In addition to these factors, consumers can now easily hear the entirety of a new album online, which – unfortunately, in the case of numerous artists – may lead the listener to conclude that there are two or three good tracks and the rest are rubbish, so why buy the whole thing?

Recent statistics suggest that, after several years in the doldrums, the UK industry may be turning the corner. Album sales in the year ending September 2004 stand at a record high of 237 million units, and there is strong growth in legal downloads coupled with a downturn in illegal file sharing. Hopefully, the worst of the job-cutting is over and companies are facing the future as leaner and more efficient businesses.

The UK industry is therefore in the throes of radical change in the early years of the 21st century. It is both battling with and embracing new technology and media, looking forward to the future whilst simultaneously fighting a late rearguard action to extend the life of copyright beyond the period of 50 years from the creation of particular recordings, an anomaly which is now threatening income streams from the early rock 'n' roll recordings. The rewards for signing successful new artists have never been greater, yet the reliance upon back-catalogue exploitation is constantly growing. And ultimately, the uncertainty that the industry faces will be reflected in the career prospects for all new artists, songwriters and managers.

## This Book

The purpose of this book is twofold: firstly, to give the reader an insight into how the different areas of the UK music business work, and secondly, to give advice and suggestions on how best to go about getting a record deal or, indeed, a publishing deal or management. Often, this advice will be based on what not to do. This second edition of The Band's Guide To Getting A Record Deal will be angled as much towards those who wish to get involved in artist management as towards artists and songwriters.

I think that it may be helpful if I tell you a little about my own background in the industry, as it may help to explain some of the views I will be putting forward later. It may also illustrate some of the highs and lows that a life in the music business can involve and will, hopefully, mean that I can connect with the reader as a result of some shared experiences.

I would be the first to admit that I am hardly a shining example of a music industry success, but hopefully the ups and downs I have experienced have given me the grounding to be able to put the industry in perspective for others. All my views are, of course, personal and subjective, but I have tried to be as fair to the business as I can. If there is a moral to the book, it is that there is no right answer in trying to get signed – but there are a lot of wrong ways to go about the early stages of your career which make getting signed less likely. As you're about to discover, sometimes getting signed is only the start of the battle.

It is also true to say that, over the last few years, the landscape of the industry has changed irrevocably, to the extent that it is less clear than ever what a 'record deal' actually amounts to. One simple truth that has emerged is that it is now easier than it has ever been to market and sell your music, without that necessarily being a passport to riches and fame. It can be only a good thing that the industry is less of a closed shop than it was – although the flipside is that there is a danger of truly special artists being lost in a huge morass of downloads, websites and online media.

Some parts of this book are, not to put too fine a point on it, a bit dull. Unfortunately, there is no exciting way to describe royalty accounting! I've assumed that the reader is either a musician, a songwriter or a manager, or perhaps someone who is generally interested in the industry perhaps from a career point of view. To those readers who are some way up the ladder, some of the advice will seem simplistic, blindingly obvious or just plain common sense. However, I have based my pitch on some of the questions I have been asked on my travels, all of which implied a fairly sketchy knowledge of the inner workings of the industry.

As they say, knowledge is power, so I hope you manage to wade through the whole book to get the whole picture. There is no substitute for actual talent, ambition and ability, however, so I'm assuming that the reader has them by the bucketload!

I never had any particular intention to end up working in the music business. I played guitar, I was obsessed with music and I spent most of my spare cash on singles, but I had no real understanding of the industry itself. I looked at record sleeves and labels and knew all the names of the record companies, but like most teenagers it was the bands and the songs that swept me away. Most of the singles and albums I bought tended to be second hand, and gradually I began to identify certain labels with certain genres: Vertigo tended to be rock, and Virgin tended to be something either punky or leftfield, while Harvest tended to be progressive.

I didn't really connect with the idea that somewhere, in an office in London, people worked for these labels and were making decisions about the bands I was obsessed with. There was little or no information available about the industry, or even about the bands themselves, unless you bought Melody Maker, Record Mirror, the NME and Sounds every week. Bigger bands tended to have fan clubs which, if you joined them, would send you a poorly photocopied magazine every few months and maybe a scrap of paper with some 'advance warning' of tour dates. It was all a bit primitive. These days, as soon as somebody in my favourite bands blows their nose, I get an email…

The turning point came when I was studying Law at Leeds University in the early 1980s. I had decided to take a Law degree only because my A-levels were (apparently) suitable for the subject, my best friend had decided to do it and I couldn't think of anything else to do. So in 1981 I was to be found driving my flatmates insane with an £80 CSl guitar/effects box combination (the effects controls were actually on the guitar – weird) and cheap practice amp, playing along to anything I could, with varying degrees of success. To make up for the unremitting dullness of its Law course, Leeds University at that time had the reputation for having one of the best gig venues in the country, with major bands playing in the Refectory most weeks and smaller gigs almost every night. The booking policy for bands was controlled by the Ents section of the Students' Union, and at that time the Ents Secretary was a garrulous northerner called Andy Kershaw. I wonder what happened to him...?

I got into the habit of sitting up in the gallery of the Refectory on gig afternoons, ostensibly studying but in fact watching the bands set up, trying to work out how the PA, lights and backline all connected, and coveting every single guitar that was brought onto the stage. I soon ended up 'humping' after gigs for the Ents crew. The deal was simple: for the privilege of straining every muscle in your body lifting gigantic flightcases into the backs of trucks at 1am in the pissing sleet, helping out the band's crew, you got some (usually warm) lager and a bit of reflected glory. The best night by far was a show by U2, who arrived late after driving down from doing *The Tube* live in Newcastle and opened their set with 'Gloria', with Bono at the height of his flag-waving period.

I soon decided to join a band, even though my gear – and some might say my playing – was fairly crap. So I took the traditional route of putting up a notice on the Students' Union board, the usual 'Guitarist seeks band into...blah blah'. I auditioned for a few, all of which were either totally useless or leagues ahead of me. I remember one audition that involved playing the riff from 'Smoke On The Water' for approximately 30 minutes continuously. I turned that one down.

At the time, I was very into so-called AOR ('adult-oriented rock', as it was known), usually perpetrated by American bands with ludicrous bouffant hairstyles and medically inadvisable trousers. Early Van Halen, Journey and (perhaps most unforgivably) Kansas were the prime suspects on my tape player. This was pre-CD. Yes, I am actually that old.

One evening, I got a call from a guy called Sammy (I later found out that his real name was Ian), who was the lead singer/bass player for a fairly well-known local rock band called East To West. Strictly speaking, they were from Pudsey, but I didn't hold that against them. They were looking for a second guitarist. They were AOR rock/pop in their influences so I decided to go and watch them rehearse and maybe have a jam with them. I turned up at the hall where they held their rehearsals after a long bus ride with my newly acquired Fender Strat (white lacquer, black scratchplate, maple neck – very nice) and my minuscule practice amp. I wasn't prepared for the mass of Marshall and Peavey stacks that greeted me, nor for the three bouffanted lads with painful-looking trousers who were horrified at my rather unfortunate geeky law-student attire. I sat at the back as they ran through their set. They were frighteningly good – three-part harmonies, great songs, good looks – and I knew straight away that there was no point even plugging my guitar in. The drummer even had a headset mic – these boys were serious. I said I'd come to see them at their next gig, at a student hall of residence the following week. They gave me a cassette that they sold at gigs.

I went to the gig and they totally blew me away. It was packed, not least with women in a variety of rock-chick outfits, which only made things more interesting. The band were playing the gig only because they couldn't get out of it and didn't really want to do it as a three-piece. I got a lift back with Sammy and his dad, and I started asking questions. Apart from their tape, the band hadn't got a photo, a biography or business cards, and they booked their own gigs at a circuit of pubs and clubs where they had played for a few years. Sammy's dad handled what little organisation there was. I couldn't get the band out of my mind, and when Sammy called me a few days later to ask if I wanted to audition properly, I said that I didn't think I was good enough, before uttering the fateful words, 'Er…have you got a manager?'

Three years later, I was still managing the band. They were then called Arena, a superb rock four-piece with twin guitars, touring the rock clubs of the UK and building up a little following. The press had started to review the band, and we'd pressed up 1,000 copies of a vinyl single that we sold at gigs. We had photos, biogs, a mailing list and T-shirts. I booked the shows and handled the organisational side (I'd bought myself a typewriter!).

As the band got bigger, *Kerrang!* started to take notice, and a brilliant journalist called Mark Putterford (RIP) began to write some nice stuff about us, including a feature in the *Kerrang!* Yearbook of 1985 as 'one to watch' for the coming year. We sold out the Marquee in London a couple of times by running coach trips from Leeds for the band's fans, and we even did a few shows in Paris.

Managing the band was a bit of a cottage industry. Back in those days there were no mobile phones, no personal computers (and, of course, no email), no faxes and no CDs. Even photocopying was a mysterious and expensive new technology. I did what business I could from the payphone near my flat and by post, and by using the revolutionary method of getting on a bus and going to see people. I got local journalists on side, blagged support gigs from bigger bands, and every time the band did anything of note I issued a press release.

Arena never really got close to a record deal, apart from a few demos for some labels, and the band eventually imploded; a couple of the guys left to get real jobs, lives and sensible girlfriends, and eventually I found myself managing the new singer as a solo artist.

By this time I was working at EMI. I had got gradually more convinced whilst at Leeds that I simply didn't want to be a solicitor. Whilst everyone else in the lecture theatre was reading The Times' Law Reports and practising wearing Pringle tanktops, I tended to be reading the NME and scheming and plotting the next move for the band. A chance remark from my dad when discussing my dilemma – 'Surely, record companies must have legal departments?' – had seen a lightbulb of gigantic wattage come on, and I began to bombard all the London record companies with my CV. I used to get the addresses from the London *Yellow Pages* in the University library, until I realised that most of the information given was either out of date or the addresses of record-pressing plants. As I say, information was fairly scant.

Eventually I got in to see EMI, and luckily they had a job going as a contracts drafter in the Business Affairs Department, the part of the company that dealt with the contractual and legal side of the business, and I moved to London in the summer of 1985. The first bit of paper I got across my desk at EMI was a letter about buying Duran Duran some new equipment – amazing stuff to look at, considering that the week before I had been weighed down with legal books in Leeds. The office was in the famous EMI Building at 20 Manchester Square, where the timeless photographs of The Beatles leaning over the balcony on the 'Red' and 'Blue' albums were taken.

EMI seemed fairly cool about me still dabbling in management. The singer in Arena, Mark, had a lot of new songs which I thought were great, and we set about demoing them in a studio in Dewsbury, with a mate of mine producing the sessions. Mark was a bit of a mystery; for instance, I could never get through to him on the phone after about 8pm. He told me that his number was similar to the number of the local cab firm, so he took it off the hook at night. He was (apparently) 26 and, although married, seemed 100% committed to making a go of the business. Naively, I negotiated a management deal with him, but never got around to signing it. As the sessions went on, things started to get expensive – studio time, photo sessions, musicians and so on – but this was the mid-'80s and so I had every credit card possible, all up to their limit, plus a growing overdraft. Eventually I got a second mortgage on my flat for £10,000, which just about covered what I had spent.

Things soon went sour as Mark realised I had run out of money. We pressed up a promotional EP on our own label to try to generate some interest, and we got close to a publishing deal with a small publishing house that eventually went on to sign The Spice Girls (probably a better move on their part, in retrospect!). I discovered that Mark was actually 30 and had three young kids (hence the phone not being allowed to wake them in the evening), we had a huge falling-out and he told me that he was giving up the business for good. A year later, I found out that he had instead just latched onto someone else with some cash. Apparently he never got a deal and ended up in a Bee Gees tribute act.

I resolved to never manage anyone again.

I knuckled down to the EMI job and had a whale of a time – a couple of free gigs a week, free CDs, overseas trips and so on. I became head of Business Affairs for EMI's video division, and things were looking rosy. I was well on my way to becoming a solid EMI company man, complete with the shiny new Cavalier and corporate American Express card.

A few years later, I was to be found drinking a cup of tea on the steps of the Amphitheatre in Verona, watching my new band Twentynine Palms soundcheck before supporting Sting in front of 15,000 people. A girl I knew from school had rung me (in my semi-mythical capacity as the only person from York ever to get a job at a record company) and said that her new boyfriend had a tape, and asked if would I listen to it. It was brilliant, sort of Van Morrison meets The Hothouse Flowers meets Elvis Costello, but with some unique lyrical and vocal twists that really made it stand out. It turned out that Simon, the singer, had some interest already, and so this time I took the plunge and signed a proper management deal with the band.

The band was effectively a duo, Simon and his cousin Davy, who played guitar. It had no name, apart from 'Simon And Davy', although we were toying with the name Never You Mind (as in 'What's your band called?' 'Never you mind.' 'All right, I was only asking...'). Simon called me one day in a state of high excitement – Miles Copeland, who was Sting's manager and owned his own record company, called IRS, had called him and offered him a record and publishing deal and had told him to get a lawyer.

Things moved quickly. We got a guy called John Kennedy to be the band's lawyer, on the basis that he was the lawyer who had asked me the most difficult questions over the years when I had been doing deals with him. The deal wasn't massively lucrative: an advance of £15,000 for an album, plus recording costs, and another £15,000 for the publishing. We hesitated on signing, as we had a few other publishers interested, but then took the plunge and signed with IRS as they were prepared to record an album straight away.

At the time, IRS was a well-established company with a worldwide link with EMI, through which it released its product. Its main claim to fame was that it had signed REM ten years earlier and owned their acclaimed early albums. Even then, it had bands such as The Alarm and Black Sabbath signed to it, with a total roster of about 15 artists. We went over to Los Angeles and were treated royally, and felt that the company, although small, was really committed to us and would do anything it could to break the band.

Miles was (and is) a mercurial and legendary character who specialises in keeping as many balls in the air as possible. Just when you thought he'd completely forgotten you, the phone would ring and a tirade of Miles-ese would pour forth – ideas (some of them brilliant and some of them mad), insults, praise and promises (some of which were actually fulfilled – a rarity in the music business). We got on with recording the album at a lovely residential studio called the Chapel, in Lincolnshire, after getting the songs into shape on a long UK tour supporting Jools Holland (another of Miles's clients) around the UK.

Incredibly in retrospect, IRS allowed the band to produce the album themselves, and luckily it turned out to be a very impressive debut (naturally, I am biased). In the end, certain key tracks were mixed by Van Morrison's engineer, Mick Glossop, who transformed them completely into serious radio contenders. By this stage, the band had settled on the name Twentynine Palms, after a little town in the desert outside LA that we ended up visiting. The album, *Fatal Joy*, was released to a wall of indifference after a single, 'Magic Man', did reasonably well at radio stations. I will never forget the first time I heard it on the radio: Richard Skinner played it on Radio 1 on a Saturday afternoon. Although I knew it was going to be played, I still nearly drove into a ditch when it was!

Most of the time we dealt with Steve Tannett, the head of IRS in the UK, with whom we got on really well. Steve understood the band's influences, sense of humour and songwriting, and most importantly he understood the concept of artist development. The American end of IRS was where we began to have problems – on creative issues such as artwork, and also on tour funding. The band needed three session musicians with them to tour, and they weren't outrageously expensive, but it still meant that every gig cost us (ie IRS, because they were fronting the money) about £300 to do. Our argument was that we needed to build up a live following and, once we had done that, we would be able to tour without needing IRS's money.

I soon realised that my experience of management up to this point had been negligible. This was full-on stuff, with constant rows about money and strategy, and only the benefit of a hugely talented and good-humoured band as the upside. Simon and Davy tended to view the antics of the label with a kind of resigned stoicism. All artists, I think, reach a point very soon after signing a deal when they realise that people with wildly diverging opinions and agendas suddenly have something to say about their career, for the simple reasons that they are investing the money and think they know best, a lot of the time.

Essentially, the Americans believed that we would never break in the UK, and that the USA was our ideal market. We toured over there, playing at various EMI Distribution conventions, and went down a storm. IRS suggested a 50-date club tour, which would have cost about $50,000 to do and taken three months. We looked at the dates and decided we wouldn't do it – partly because we weren't convinced that anyone would come to the shows, or that IRS would be capable of building any kind of a marketing campaign around the album, but equally because the band didn't want to spend that amount of time away from home for personal reasons.

It is fair to say that IRS went nuts when we told them we didn't want to do the tour, and from that moment on the American end of the record company always considered us 'difficult', and concentrated their efforts on acts that weren't. It was a mistake; we should have done it.

Instead, we played around the clubs of the UK with little support from IRS for a second single, a huge ballad which could have been a hit with the right breaks. Our option was coming up and, although the new songs were even better than the older material, we felt that we were likely to be dropped as the first album hadn't done too well, apart from in places like Germany and France. However, EMI liked us and seemed to think that IRS could have a major band on their hands if the next album was rockier and a bit less folky. One day the phone rang and it was Miles, casually asking if we wanted to support Sting on his six-week summer European tour, which started in two weeks' time. To say that we jumped at the chance is putting it mildly. All the EMI Europe companies in the countries that the tour would visit vowed to give *Fatal Joy* another push. We hastily assembled a crew and a cheap splitter van, booked hotels and set off to the first show in Lausanne, Switzerland.

The tour would end up visiting Italy, Germany, Austria, France and Spain. We were nervous, but everything turned out to be fine. Nothing was too much trouble for Sting's crew (they even trucked our gear), and there were a lot of really nice moments. One came when, after the first show (where we had gone down really well), Simon was summoned to Sting's dressing room by his glowering tour manager. I instantly assumed that we would be thrown off the tour if we kept going down as well as we had done, but in fact Sting asked Simon if he would come on during his set and sing 'Every Breath You Take' with him every night. Which was nice!

There was little or no rock-star bullshit about Sting. He ate with the crew, had a laugh, worked hard, and got paid barrel-loads of money in the process. Fair play to him.

We soon realised that EMI Europe were not pulling their weight as IRS's European licensees. We would be playing to between 15,000 and 20,000 people a night, and going down great, yet none of the record shops in the cities we played in had the album. This is the kind of thing that drives all bands and managers demented. I would have the band go and say hello to the audience at the merchandise desk after their set, sign stuff and get their picture taken, in the grim knowledge that it was highly unlikely that anyone in Lyon, Vicenza or Barcelona would stand a chance of finding the album. These days, of course, they would order it online and have it delivered in a few days.

Obviously the tour happened at short notice, but our noses were distinctly out of joint as we knew that the audiences who saw us liked us – even though none of them were able to say 'Twentynine Palms' or knew what it meant. (Another lesson learned: try to have a short band name that everyone can pronounce. It helps!) By this time I had left EMI and was working for a big TV company as a lawyer, which gave me more time to manage the band.

Amazingly, despite the tour not having led to a massive increase in sales for the first album, IRS picked up the option for another record and committed a recording budget to it that was large by any label's standards. We had felt on the tour that some of the gentler songs from the first album hadn't really stood up to larger gigs, and so the new songs had moved in a rockier direction. This time, Mick Glossop was drafted in to produce the whole record, as we were looking for that epic, folk-rock sound he had given The Waterboys when he produced 'The Whole Of The Moon'. The budget was over £100,000, and we thoroughly enjoyed spending every penny! The album, No Eden, was everything we had hoped for, and the band and IRS thought that the time had come to break into the big league.

It was not to be. In the interim, IRS had been fully bought out by EMI and now had little control (outside the USA) over which of their albums and bands were to be given priority, and in some cases which were to be released at all. All of a sudden, IRS weren't calling the shots anymore, and we felt that they (and we) were in the position of having to convince EMI to get behind the band. It was almost like having just been signed again, despite all the hard work that we and IRS had put in.

To be honest, EMI had enough of their own bands to work on without spending time, money and resources on a band signed to a little label they had just bought. They released a couple of half-hearted singles, bought us some nice lunches and we did a bit more touring, but EMI's heart wasn't in it. Steve Tannett, so used to translating to us some of the more bizarre ideas coming out of IRS America, could do little more as his hands were tied. It was a depressing and frustrating time for all of us, especially as the album got great reviews and we were now starting to build quite a live following, helped by tours with Joe Cocker and Squeeze.

Soon the tour support funding dried up and the band toured as a duo plus keyboard player in the USA and Canada, which was ironic considering that the new album was a full-on rock record and that it was the first album's more acoustic vibe that would have lent itself to the three-piece format. The frustration got to Davy more than anyone, as he was the band's Mr Logical and couldn't understand why the record company would get things so close to a breakthrough and then not see it through. He quit the band after the final round of club dates (the official reason was that he 'wanted to move to India and grow a beard in peace', which is Davy-speak for 'this industry is run by idiots'). I assumed that it was all over and that we would be dropped.

Unbelievably, IRS picked up the next option after putting the band's contract into suspension, as they were entitled to do if someone left. Simon built a new band around him, The Libertines (yes, The Libertines, we thought of it first, although because there was another band in the USA with the same name we had to change it to 'The Last Libertines' over there), and a low-budget album was recorded. We toured around the clubs for a year at a pittance, until eventually IRS were forced to put the record out with no help from EMI.

Effectively, this meant that they pressed a few thousand, took a few ads and got the record into the shops. To this day I have no idea why they ever picked up the option, as they put nothing behind the release of the record and only succeeded in building up even more of a debt on the band's debit balance. Soon afterwards, the inevitable happened and The Libertines were dropped, although IRS kept Simon signed for publishing. He later went on to write songs covered by Zucchero and Paul Young.

To anyone – especially those trying to get a record deal – getting a band signed to a record label and actually keeping it going for three albums would be some kind of an achievement. But the frustration of being so close and yet so far, despite having some great times along the way, was an incredibly bruising experience.

I resolved, once more, never to manage anyone again.

Instead, I set up a video production company and produced promo clips, documentaries and live concert videos for artists such as Paul Weller, Sting, The Cardigans, Ant And Dec, Def Leppard, Metallica, Phil Collins and, possibly most exciting of all, Max Bygraves.

A few months ago, I was to be found in a packed rock club in downtown Tokyo watching one of our new bands go down a storm and then sign autographs for an hour after the show. All that stuff about never managing anyone again? Who said that?

So after all that long-winded waffle, do you still want to get signed? I thought so – then read on. After all, it's better than digging a ditch...

# Joke 1

A blind snake and a blind rabbit bump into each other on a jungle path. The rabbit says, 'Excuse me, mate, could you do me a favour and feel me all over, and tell me what I am? I'm blind.' The snake says, 'All right, but you've got to do the same for me because I'm blind as well.' The rabbit agrees and the snake slides all over him, feeling every nook and cranny. Eventually the snake says, 'Well, you're furry, with two big floppy ears and a little bob tail. I reckon you're a rabbit.' The rabbit hops all over the snake, prodding it with his paws, looking confused. Eventually he says, 'As far as I can work out, you're slimy, nearly deaf and everyone hates you. You're an A&R man!'

# Joke 2

A man is walking through a field in the fog when he hears a voice shouting 'Hello, can you tell me where I am?' He looks up and there is a balloon hovering 20 feet above him. The balloonist shouts again, 'Have you got any idea where I am?' The guy on the ground thinks for a moment and says, 'Well...you're in a balloon hovering 20 feet above this field.' Exasperated, the balloonist shouts, 'I bet you manage bands. What you've just told me is totally accurate, but of no use to me whatsoever'. The man on the ground retorts, 'I do manage bands and I assume you're in a band – you've got no idea where you are, or where you're going, but apparently now it's all my fault.'

# CHAPTER 1

# WHAT IS A RECORD DEAL?

## Introduction

You are probably reading this because you want a record deal, either from the perspective of being an artist or perhaps as an artist manager. So the best way to start is to understand exactly what a 'record deal' is, and what being 'signed' to a record company means.

A record deal – or, to express it more formally, a recording contract – is an agreement between an artist and a record company or production company. For the purposes of this chapter, we will treat record companies and production companies as the same entity, although there can be significant differences in the way in which they operate.

A recording contract is a legally binding document, usually prepared by the record company and then negotiated between the record company's solicitors and the artist's solicitors or management.

The prime purpose of any recording contract is to give the record company certain 'rights' to exploit (ie use, or sell) recordings of the artist's performances. The contract will provide that these recordings are either made by the record company, or made by the artist and then licensed from the artist to the record company. The most common example of 'exploitation' of recordings is selling them on formats such as compact disc, vinyl, DVD and MiniDisc, through retailers. Record companies, amongst others, also exploit recordings as downloads. An example of 'exploitation' would be the use of a recording in the soundtrack of a film or an advert.

The point here is that record deals do not concern songs, but recordings of songs. Songwriters are signed to publishing companies, who deal with the exploitation of songs and not recordings, under the terms of publishing agreements.

It is crucial to understand the difference between a recording and a song. Record companies deal with recordings.

# The Purpose Of A Recording Contract

A standard recording contract from a major record company can be around 60 pages long. These documents have evolved over many years of negotiation between record companies and artists, and their length reflects the complexity of the modern music business. That's not to say that a valid record deal can't be signed on the back of a fag packet in a pub; it's just that it's not a particularly good idea!

Legal cases over recent years have had a huge impact on recording contracts and their enforceability. Some of the cases – Holly Johnson and ZTT, The Stone Roses and Silvertone, George Michael and Sony – have forced record companies to redraft their recording contracts to ensure their legality. It is fair to say that most (but not all) disputes between record companies and artists have been resolved in the favour of the artist. Historically, recording contracts have been hugely biased in favour of the record companies, and to a lesser extent they still are. It is not uncommon even today for legendary stars of the '60s and '70s still to be paid on the terms of their original recording contract, for royalties which might be as low as a few old pence per track.

Even a layman looking at a standard recording contract might notice a few startling aspects to it. Let's take compact discs – the format on which most of the world's music is sold – as an example. You might be forgiven for thinking that royalties paid to artists on sales of CDs were calculated on the price at which the CD was sold, either to the record shop or the consumer. Yet, throughout the 1980s and beyond, many record companies paid royalties on CD sales based on the retail or dealer prices of ordinary vinyl albums, which sold at getting on for half the price of CDs! Incredibly, some record companies' first negotiating position even today is to offer to pay on the black-vinyl price.

As a result of the increased profit margins gained, the artists and the public effectively paid for the record companies' shiny new CD-manufacturing plants through the back door.

In recent years, most major record companies have been getting extremely worked up about the principle of earning income from every possible aspect of an artist's career. The first battleground has been downloads, with record companies slowly waking up to the potential of enormous income being derived from online exploitation of their artist's recordings. Assuming that record companies have the right to do this – and in certain recording agreements it is by no means certain that these rights were ever granted – then all record companies have been examining ways of paying their artists the lowest royalties they can possibly get away with for each download. As part of the music industry's painfully slow awakening to the positive aspects of online exploitation, they have realised that the traditional models of exploitation of albums, singles and even CDs are coming to an end, and perhaps the lack of physical product (huge warehouses full of CDs) isn't altogether a bad thing – just as long as they can extract as much money out of the brave new world as possible.

Many major record companies are also now seeking to grab a piece of the income an artist makes from areas other than recordings, particularly merchandising and income derived from the artist's website. There is a strong feeling amongst the majors that they have 'created' the artist (at one recent meeting, a major-label executive described one of their artists to me as a 'brand') and therefore deserve a taste of each slice of the pie representing the artist's sources of income. Needless to say, artist managers are either embracing these ideas to a certain extent – witness the recent Robbie Williams/EMI deal – or resisting them as much as possible, reasoning that any encroachment by the record companies on these areas (unless accompanied by a large cheque) is bound to reduce an artist's income by the back door..

One bizarre facet of recording contracts concerns the actual number of records sold upon which royalties are calculated. Surely, you might think, artists get paid on all the sales that are made? Not so. Some record companies still pay on only 90% of the total number of records sold – an historical anomaly dating back to the days of brittle 78rpm vinyl records, 10% of which broke on their journey from the pressing plant to the shop! Needless to say, record companies have not been eager to update this kind of area.

Although record companies generously pay for the actual manufacturing costs of the various formats, such as CD, they almost invariably take a so-called 'packaging deduction' from the artist royalty, supposedly to cover the CD or case and inlay card, or cardboard sleeve. These packaging deductions bear no relation whatsoever to the actual cost of these items. And guess what? The record companies deduct huge amounts more than they actually cost.

# It Gets Worse...

Probably the single most outrageous aspect of all standard recording contracts concerns copyright and the ownership of master recordings. The costs of recording a single or an album are paid for upfront by record companies, but are charged in full to each artist's royalty account. The royalty account thus has a 'debit balance', rather like a bank overdraft, although the sums an artist owes a record company are not repayable personally as though they were a debt; instead, they are paid back, or 'recouped', from the artist's royalties. In other words, the artist will not actually receive any royalties from sales of his records until his debit balance has recouped.

Sums that are to be paid back from the artist's royalties are known as 'recoupable' sums. If insufficient royalties arise to recoup the debit balance, and the record company then parts company with the artist, the amount owed is not repayable by the artist, but any future royalties generated by the artist for the company will still go to pay off the debit.

However, take a situation where the artist has recouped. Let's assume that a record company has spent £100,000 making an album and paying an advance to the artist. The artist's royalty, after all deductions, works out at £0.75 per CD. The CD sells 133,334 copies. Result: recoupment! So the artist has paid back all the recoupable costs that the record company has 'lent' him. But who owns the copyright in the album?

# The Record Company!

But surely, if the artist has paid for the album then the artist should own it? After all, your building society doesn't own your house once you've paid back the mortgage, does it? Since when do you pay for something to be made, or buy something, and then not own it? Since you signed a record deal, that's when.

# The Record Companies' Position

The record companies' view of all this goes as follows. They spend huge amounts of money on signing and developing artists that may only ever sell ten records in Albania. They spend even more money marketing and promoting the successful artists they do have and trying to develop their long-term careers. They reinvest their profits constantly in new talent, and they play a major part in the cultural life of the nation, as well as bringing huge amounts of overseas income into the UK. They are companies like any other company, and have a duty to make a profit for their shareholders.

It is only fair to point out here that in recent years some record companies have made significant efforts to modernise their recording contracts, and in some cases they offer to give recordings back to the artists after a certain number of years have passed following the end of the deal, or they have got rid of packaging deductions. However, such progressive thinking in some areas has usually been accompanied by stricter provisions in others – lower royalty rates, tightly controlled tour support and so on.

In the final analysis, record companies are in the business of creating, owning and exploiting recordings, and they will fight tooth and nail to retain ownership of the rights in those recordings.

A cynic's view would be that the prime purpose of a recording contract is to tie an artist to the record company for as long as possible, pay them as little as possible and exploit as many copyrights generated by that artist by every method possible and for as long as possible.

# The Terms Of A Recording Contract

The main terms of a recording contract will specify:

(i) How many recordings the artist is required to deliver to the record company (such as one single, or a whole album) and the ways in which the record company can exploit the recordings;

(ii) That the record company will have a number of options, on its side, to require the artist to deliver more recordings, in the form of further singles or albums;

(iii) What royalties the record company will pay to the artist when it sells the recordings, how often it will pay these royalties, and on what basis the royalties are calculated;

(iv) What territories the record company is allowed to exploit the recordings in;

(v) What advances (ie money) the record company will give the artist against royalties, and in what instalments these advances will be paid;

(vi) What costs (such as advances, recording costs, video costs or tour support) the record company will pay itself back ('recoup') from royalties before the artist actually receives royalty payments.

# The Detail

Your attention may be flagging a bit at this point. Once we've got over this next part, which is possibly the dullest in the book, things will get more exciting.

We need to look at the finer detail of recording contracts, so I apologise if some of what follows seems baffling at first, but it serves to illustrate the complexity of these agreements and the lengths to which record companies will go to protect their rights.

The more you understand, the more questions you can ask your manager or lawyer.

## (i) Definitions

The first few pages of any recording contract usually deal with the definitions of words to be found in the main body of the agreement. As the contract will deal with some extremely technical areas, terms such as 'record' and 'compact disc' will be defined precisely.

One key definition concerns the detail of what 'delivery' by the artist to the company amounts to, as delivering recordings is of the essence of the agreement.

One definition which often causes amusement is 'the Territory'. In the case of a worldwide deal, the territory will usually be defined as 'the World and the Solar System' – not, as you might think, because the rent for a pressing plant is cheaper on Mars, but to cover satellite transmissions of copyright material owned by the record company.

Modern recording contracts will now define DVDs, mobile applications, downloads, online sales and other terms relating to new technology in tremendous detail.

## (ii) The Term And Minimum Commitment

The 'Term' means how long the contract can last for.

Following the ZTT vs Holly Johnson case in 1989, record companies were forced to reassess urgently the wording of their contracts. In simple terms, the Holly Johnson case means that record companies can no longer bind artists to extremely long contracts without there being quite stringent obligations upon the record company to develop the artist's career.

Any record company is likely to want to commit an artist to record one album (singles-only deals with major record companies are now almost non-existent, except for dance tracks) followed by five or six options for one further album each. The date upon which the record company has to pick up each option will normally relate to a period – say, six months – following the release of the previous album. (Some record companies will exclude the months of November and December from the calculation of this period, as most albums will already have been released before this peak sales period.) To avoid the prospect of the company forgetting to pick up an option and thus losing the artist (it does happen), many contracts now provide that, at the and of any period, the next option is deemed to be picked up unless the company specifically informs the artist it is not going to do so.

These contract periods will usually be referred to as the 'Initial Period' followed by the 'First Option Period', 'Second Option Period' and so on. So, when you hear of a band signing a 'six-album deal', in all likelihood the company has committed to only one album, with future product on option. In rare instances, a company will commit to a 'two albums firm' deal, guaranteeing to record a minimum of two albums. This is a sign of enormous commitment from a record company and suggests that they have managed to sign the artist after a bidding war with other labels. In most cases, however, the 'Minimum Commitment' in each period will be an album.

The nightmare scenario that can develop is that an artist can have the particular contract period that they are in at any one time extended for a variety of reasons. It could be that their A&R person is not happy with the demos submitted for the new album, or that they are waiting for a particular producer to become available, or that a member of the band has left. Most lawyers acting for artists will insist that no contract period is permitted to last longer than two years, under any circumstances, and will also insist that, if the record company asks for an extension, they will advance further money to the artist.

It is important to note at this point that, in many contracts, the record company will not guarantee to release the artist's album at all; instead, release hinges on 'acceptance' by the company. In other words, the company can reject delivery of an album by relying on quite precise conditions contained in the contract. The company will want the contract to say that each album must be 'commercially acceptable' – one of the vaguest terms in any record deal. A good lawyer acting for the artist should be able to tone this down to 'technically acceptable'.

If the album delivered by the artist is accepted, most companies will now agree a 'release commitment'. In other words, they will guarantee to release the album in as few major territories as they can get away with. From the company's point of view, if they have international branches, there is no guarantee that their overseas partners will be as interested in releasing the album in question as they are. Record companies are traditionally extremely wary of release commitments.

One downside of release commitments is that, although the artist will now have the security of knowing that his work will definitely be released, the record company is likely to want to tie the next option date to the release date, rather than the earlier delivery date. In other words, the price for a release commitment may well be that a contractual period lasts longer.

## (iii) Exclusivity, Grant Of Rights And Copyright

Record companies need to ensure that the artist is restricted to making records and videos only for them. Artists will usually be permitted to appear as guests on other artists records, but only if their record company receives a credit (eg, '...appears by kind permission of...') and sometimes even a fee or a so-called 'override' royalty from whichever record company is releasing the record upon which their artist guests.

Usually, the contract will state that the artist is allowed to have his 'performances' (which may be defined as including speech) recorded by TV and radio companies as long as the recordings are not made available commercially without the record company's consent. In addition, the artist may be required to take some steps to stop his concerts being 'bootlegged' (ie illegally recorded and sold).

In addition, the company will impose a 're-recording restriction' on the artist. For a period following the termination of the agreement (usually at least five years), the artist will be prevented from re-recording any of the tracks recorded for the company, for another company. Although this provision is primarily designed to stop another company from reaping the benefit of a re-recorded hit that the original record company had, it can have another, detrimental effect on artists. If an artist is dropped by a label which has refused to release the artist's latest album, the artist may not be able to re-record any of the unreleased tracks in order to gain a new record deal with another company. Most artist lawyers thus insist that the re-recording restriction applies only to recordings actually released by the original company during the original agreement, or within a short time afterwards.

The copyright in all recordings made under the provisions of the contract will almost invariably be granted to the company by the artist, along with the right for the company to use the artist's name and image in exploiting the recordings. These rights will usually be granted for the full life of copyright. The company will be granted the unlimited and exclusive right to manufacture, distribute and sell records derived from the recordings, and the right to license other companies to do so. The company will also be granted the right to do none of the foregoing if it chooses not to.

The bottom line is essentially that the company wants to do almost anything one might conceivably imagine with the recordings delivered to it.

## (iv) Advances, Royalties And Recording Costs

In a standard recording contract, the advances (ie payments) in each contract period are usually paid in instalments of 50% on signature of the deal (or exercise of an option) and 50% on delivery of the 'Minimum Commitment' (usually an album) for that contract period. Such arrangements can vary greatly from deal to deal; a company may agree to pay the majority of the advance for the period in a lump sum, part of it on commencement of recording an album, or in monthly instalments.

Advances will rise with each subsequent contract period, slowly at first and then on a steeper curve. In reality, once an artist has become successful and has perhaps recouped, the entire advance and royalty structure of the deal will be aggressively renegotiated upwards by lawyers acting for the artist. Often, the press make a huge song and dance about bands who have supposedly signed a deal said to be worth millions. These stories should always be taken with a pinch of salt. Clearly, if all the advances and recording costs under a healthy record deal were added up, they might exceed £1 million, but this suggests that the band will have every option picked up by the company. On a six-album deal, this is likely to take the best part of a decade!

It may sound extremely impressive if a band you know of signs a deal where the initial advance is, say, £75,000 plus recording costs, but look more closely. In the case of a five-piece band, they will be left with £60,000 if their manager commissions the advance at 20%. So that's £12,000 each, less tax, which may have to last them 18 months – about £130 a week. So, unless the band can generate other income – for example, by signing a publishing deal, a merchandising deal or touring at a profit – it's hardly time to visit the local Porsche dealer! On the other hand, it's better than working for a living…

Advances for future contract periods are sometimes calculated on what is known as a 'minimax' formula, whereby the level of the advance relates to a percentage of the royalty earnings in the previous contract period. This is usually expressed as two-thirds of whatever the artist has earned in the previous period, but with a minimum of 'X' and a maximum of 'Y'. Depending on the success of the artist, either the presence of a minimum figure can be a huge comfort, or the maximum figure can be something to ignore completely during a renegotiation.

'Recording Fund' deals are also increasingly common. In these cases, the album recording budget is added to the advances to the band to give an overall sum. Effectively, the artist is allowed to 'keep the change' which has not been spent on making the album. These deals have the advantage, in theory, of pegging the company's financial commitment to a reasonably accurate level. They are also increasingly used where artists have their own studios and will be recording using their own facilities. On the downside, the financial planning implications of appearing to receive a large sum of money, the bulk of which needs to be spent on recording, should be carefully considered. All advances are recouped against royalties – in other words, they are 'advance' payments against future royalties. When they are paid, they appear on the band's debit balance along with all other recoupable amounts.

One point to note is that all advances and other recoupable costs are added together across the entire time that an artist is with a particular company, and that all royalties and income from all recordings are set against these costs. In other words, royalties from one album do not just go to pay back the costs of that album; they are 'cross-collateralised' across all royalties and income against all recoupable amounts. What this means in practical terms is that, if a band manages to become £1 million unrecouped during its Initial Period and does not sell many records, even a cheaply made but hugely successful second album selling over two million copies may not be enough to get the band out of the red with the record company.

Royalties are almost invariably based on the formula of a percentage of the 'retail' or, more usually, the 'dealer' price of records, less a huge array of possible deductions. The price at which records are sold to dealers is published in trade journals such as Music Week. For the sake of argument, the dealer price of a mainstream CD is within 50p either side of £9. From this published price, record companies offer discounts to large retail chains such as Woolworths and HMV. The price upon which the artist is paid is, surprise surprise, almost always the discounted price.

As the 'retail' price of records varies wildly from store to store, the formula used tends to be a percentage uplift of the dealer price (usually 30%) to give the notional retail price of the record. If uplifting £9 by 30% seems on the low side to you, with CDs costing up to the £15 mark in the shops, remember that the shop prices include 17.5% VAT. The published dealer price used by the record companies is the price before VAT is charged by them to the dealers.

You may wonder how it is possible for supermarkets and other major retailers to sell chart CDs at under £10. The answer is that the biggest retailers benefit from huge discounts offered by the major record companies and distributors, and are also prepared to make a very small profit margin on CDs to get the customers through their doors. All of this is bad news for independent record dealers, who protest that their loyalty to artists and labels and their support for new bands is being rewarded by an inability to compete on the price of the biggest sellers.

Further deductions are made, ranging from 10% to 30%, for the different kinds of packaging in which each format is contained – for example, cardboard sleeves, CD jewel boxes, boxed sets and so on. Any royalties payable to producers or mixers are then deducted from the artist's royalty, although a good lawyer should be able to limit the percentage paid by the artist, with the difference being swallowed by the company.

After all this, certain types of special product – for example, 12" singles, coloured vinyl discs, record-club sales, mid-price and low-price sales, and TV-advertised albums – are paid only at half or two-thirds of the contractual rate, even after all the above deductions. Again, a good lawyer should be able to set the maximum number of units to which these deductions will be applied by the company. I once worked out that, on certain formats of a hit 12" single where the producer had refused to agree to any of the same deductions as the band, the band ended up earning a royalty of –2%! In other words, for every copy sold, the band owed the record company money.

The actual percentage royalty rates vary according to a number of factors. Firstly, the format of the release – single, album, mini album and so on. Secondly, the territory – rates will usually be higher in the territory in which the artist is signed, and lower overseas, particularly where the record company does not have its own associated company. In these cases, the record company will have licensing arrangements with third-party companies and will often pay the artist a share of its 'net receipts' instead of a royalty. In other words, the company will split (usually 50/50) the money it receives from licensees with the artist. In these situations, the artist's lawyers need to impose the condition that the record company's arrangements with its licensees need to be on 'bona fide (meaning 'good faith') arm's-length commercial terms'. This means that the deal the company does with a particular licensee must be as good or better as it could have got elsewhere, and there must be no ulterior motive behind it, such as the company secretly owning part or all of the licensee.

## (v) Publishing

For a detailed explanation of the ins and outs of music publishing, please see Chapter 3, 'Music Publishing And Songwriting'. Music publishers own, control and exploit compositions written by songwriters. More often than not, the artist that a record company is signing is also a songwriter, and may already have a publishing deal. The recording contract will thus refer to 'Controlled Compositions', meaning those that have been written by the artist the record company is signing, or are owned or controlled by the artist. Record companies – amongst other users – have to pay music publishers (or, indeed, unpublished writers whose works are 'copyright control') for the use of these compositions, as the vast majority of recordings are those made of compositions controlled by publishers. For usage on records, record companies pay a so-called 'mechanical royalty' to the publishers at a rate (currently) of 8.5% of the dealer price of each record in the UK.

The majority of music publishers use 'collecting societies', such as the MCPS (Mechanical Copyright Protection Society) in the UK, to collect the income they are due, and the collecting society pays this on to its members, less a small commission. Record companies will try to minimise any payments they need to make to music publishers wherever possible in order to maximise their profit margin – for example, in America and Canada, (where a 'cent rate' per track is payable to publishers, currently 8 cents per track) record companies will usually refuse to pay the full mechanical rate and will agree to pay only 75% of the rate. In addition, the record company will try to limit the number of tracks per album they have to pay on, to a maximum of 10 or possibly 12 per CD.

Another example concerns 'synchronisation' rights, where a song is synchronised with moving images, such as a film. Normally, for usage in feature films and television programmes, the music publisher would expect to receive a significant payment. However, for songs used in promo clips (music videos), the record company will expect to receive a free or nominally priced synchronisation licence – the argument being that the showing of the clip will increase record sales and thus bring mechanical royalties to the publisher.

## (vi) Group Provisions

Record companies will insist on signing a band 'jointly and severally' – in other words, each member of the band is individually signed to the record company, and thus the company controls any solo projects outside the band. If the band splits up, it will be up to the record company which members they retain under contract and (usually) which members retain control and usage of the group name. Record companies buy themselves time to make these decisions by insisting that, in the event of a split, the contract period in force is extended for perhaps another six months, or 'suspended' for the same period.

Hugely detailed provisions cover the split of a band. As the company may have spent massive amounts of money in developing a band's career up to that point, a split can have disastrous financial consequences both for the company and the band. Recordings may have to be scrapped, tours cancelled, expensive photo sessions and promo clips consigned to the bin. Accordingly, record companies will make it extremely difficult for any key member of a band simply to walk away from the contract.

## (vii) Creative Control And Cost Control

Needless to say, most record companies are extremely wary of handing over total creative control to their artists, unless they are absolutely desperate to sign them, or the artist already has a strong track record and has demonstrated that they warrant this freedom. Most contracts will include provisions for the record company to nominate the studio, choice of material and producer, 'in consultation' with the artist.

In practice, such matters are usually resolved by mutual agreement, although disputes can often occur relating to the choice of producer. More often than not, it is impossible for the artist or the company to decide whether they have made the right choice until the recording sessions are under way.

Another potential problem area is the record company either insisting that the band record a particular track – perhaps a cover version of a song not written by the band – or refusing to fund the recording of a song that the band feel passionately about. At this point, the seeds have been sown for a dispute which may reveal that the band and the company have substantially different views about how they should proceed, creatively.

As always, there are two sides to every story. The band will feel that they should be trusted to go in whatever direction they want to go, and that the record company should stand by them. They will feel that the record company must have been impressed enough to sign them in the first place, and should not now try to rein in their creativity. The record company will not be prepared to fund recordings that it feels are likely to be neither commercially nor critically successful, nor beneficial to the band's career.

If a band are also songwriters, then a suggestion by the company that they should record some cover versions, or try working with co-writers, can be an enormous blow to the ego. Ultimately, however, the hard commercial reality is that both the company and the band are both looking for the same thing: a hit.

Have you ever noticed that, rather like people who have loads of money and profess not to care about it, the only artists who ever say they don't care about having hits are the ones who have already had quite a few?

It is very important to try to retain some control over recording costs, which the company may spend over and above the original recording budget – for example, on a series of remixes. Ideally, any artist should have the right to veto the company from remixing tracks without the artist's approval. The worst-case scenario might be that the company insists on having an entire album remixed – say, at a cost of £20,000 – because the American office of the company won't release the album otherwise. The money is spent – and then, even after the remixes, the American company still refuses to put the record out. Result: the band are a further £20,000 in hock to the company with nothing to show for it.

Another familiar example where costs can spiral out of control is promo clips (videos), where once again a clip which has been successful in the UK may be deemed unacceptable for the US market and a completely new version will have to be shot.

The artists are essentially in a no-win situation. However blunt this may sound, the most basic way in which a record company shows that it is committed to its artists is by spending a lot of money on them. If the band disagrees with certain elements of this spending, then the company may deem that they and their management are being uncooperative, and the relationship is soured.

At the end of the day, a record deal giving total creative control (and a release commitment) to the artist might mean that the record company gets to release a double album of the artist reading his shopping list, so it's little wonder that companies get a tad nervous in this area!

## (viii) Video

Music videos, known in the trade as 'promo clips', are one of the heaviest financial commitments that a record company will make to an artist. As a general rule, clips shown on, say, *Top Of The Pops* are unlikely to have been shot for a budget below £15,000. Most will have cost between £30,000 and £50,000, and the sky is the limit for bigger artists, whose shoots can command budgets of £250,000 and above. On occasion, a record company will commit to produce one or possibly two promo clips per album in the contract.

Arguments have raged for years about the recoupment of promo clip costs. Artist lawyers maintain that these clips are produced purely as marketing tools for the record company and that therefore their costs should be non-recoupable.

In the past, record companies frequently released retail video compilations of promo clips, which generated some income, but this practice is increasingly rare nowadays. Since the advent of DVD, successful artists have tended to release live concerts rather than clip compilations, not least because of the large number of clips needed to make a saleable package. So, in other words, unlike record sales, the artist might have no product in the shops from which to recoup the cost of making the promo clip.

The traditional compromise is that only half the production costs of a promo clip are recoupable against the artist's record sales, with the other half recoupable from any income arising from commercial usage of that video or other videos – ie cross-collateralised.

'Long-form videos' are usually specially filmed concerts intended for video and TV release. The record company will almost invariably wish to take from a band the rights to release these, even if the company does not have a specific division or personnel dedicated to releasing retail videos. At the very least, the company will insist on a 'right to match' any offer from another company for a long-form video. It may be possible to exclude from the record company's rights TV-only specials, which, if a band becomes successful on a worldwide scale, can be a very lucrative source of income. Whether or not the company intends to produce long-form videos, the contract will almost always set out royalty rates covering their release.

## (ix) Equipment And Tour Support

Most larger record companies are prepared to provide extra advances for touring costs, which could include the purchase of new equipment and instruments, transport, crew and production (PA and lighting). It is vital that a band includes these costs in its negotiations with a record company, particularly if they intend to tour regularly. There is great scope for creativity here – for example, a record company might agree to advance the rent on a dedicated rehearsal space in the band's home town, or on gear storage facilities, or to buy a van.

At the most mundane level, remember that, in a year of intensive gigging, a guitarist might go through hundreds of pounds' worth of strings. Who is going to pay for them? In almost all cases, the equipment purchased becomes the property of the band, and they can retain it even when their contract is terminated.

It is unlikely that the record company will agree to provide a specific sum by way of an advance for 'tour support', but they may agree a minimum sum. These negotiations will be easier if the band already has an agent (see later) who is known to the record company and already booking gigs and support slots for the band.

All record companies will want their artists to be able to tour without additional funding from them as soon as possible, but in reality only the most successful live performers are able to fund their touring needs without tour support. This tour support will be particularly necessary when the record company is insisting that the band tours to promote their product, perhaps supporting a bigger band who require a 'buy on' (see later).

It is accepted by all record companies that certain types of artists – rock artists in particular – will build their fanbase principally through touring, and the company will therefore factor in a reasonably high spend in this area during the Initial Period. However, the purse strings of the majors have become noticeably tighter in recent years and many managers are now struggling to get tours fully funded by their record companies without, for example, offering their record company their merchandising income. It may seem fantastic, as an unsigned artist, to consider the prospect of heading off on tour for weeks and months on end, but the reality of trying to live on the standard £15 per diem (the daily payment made for food and drink and personal expenses) in the motorway services of the UK is not easy, and in the past artists touring at a club level usually had the prospect of a bonus or bung from merchandise sales to keep their spirits up.

# (x) Producers

In almost all cases, producers (and some remixers and engineers) are paid by way of a royalty, against which they receive an advance, in much the same way as the artist. The point to note is that the producer's royalty is deducted from the artist's royalty, although – as stated previously – the artist may be able to specify a maximum producer's royalty that may be deducted from his royalty.

As a guideline, a 'name' producer may charge between 3% and 5% of the retail price of an album against an advance of £3,000 per track. If the producer produces only a certain number of tracks on an album, his royalty will be 'pro-rated' – that is, the number of tracks he produces will be divided by the total number of tracks on the album.

The advance to the producer will usually be treated as part of the recording costs, and thus will appear on the artist's debit balance. Ideally, the record company will not want to pay the producer his royalty until all the recording costs of the tracks he produced have been recouped, not just his advance. They are unlikely to persuade the producer's lawyers to accept this readily.

# (xi) Accounting And Audits

Stay awake at the back!

Record companies usually account to their artists every six months, within 90 days of the end of each half year in June and December. Depending on whether you're recouped or not, the receipt of your statement can be either an extremely depressing or a joyful experience, depending on the size of the figure after the minus sign or the size of the figure on the cheque! Royalty statements are tremendously detailed, setting out precisely how many records the record company claims to have sold, at what royalty base price, at what royalty rate, in which territory and by which catalogue number. The statement will also list sales of compilation albums by companies to which the record company has licensed the artist's recordings.

The statement will then total up the income due and deduct whatever recoupable costs there are, leaving a debit or credit balance.

All record companies will allow an artist's accountant to examine their books and records for the purpose of auditing the information to ascertain that the calculations are correct. Occasionally, audits do reveal discrepancies in the information, either by accident or design on behalf of the record company.

Unless an underpayment above a certain level is revealed, however, the artist will have to pay for the cost of the audit himself.

## (xii) Promotional Duties

Most record deals will contain certain provisions whereby the artist agrees to promote the release of records free of charge, other than the reimbursement of out-of-pocket expenses. Such promotion would include, for example, doing press interviews, photo sessions, appearing on radio and television and making personal appearances.

Some companies make it a contractual provision that the artist will use his 'reasonable endeavours' to tour and make TV and radio appearances in order to promote the release of records.

The record company will usually insist that any fees payable to the artist for non-tour appearances – such as Musicians' Union fees for a TV show – are instead paid directly to the company. Additionally, if the company incurs any costs as a result of the artist's failure to turn up at any such promotional events, they are likely to make such costs recoupable.

Normal paid touring work concerns the record company only if the artist requires additional advances of royalties as tour support. In this case, the record company will require sight of the budget for the tour, and will insist that all fees and sometimes even projected merchandising income are put into the pot by the band to reduce the overall tour-support bill. It is highly unlikely that the record company will make any commitment to marketing and promotion itself – for example, by agreeing to pay for a flyposter campaign for every release or by placing a certain number of advertisements in the trade press.

## (xiii) Termination

Like most contracts, there will be a provision in every record deal which will set out what happens if either party is in 'material breach' of the agreement. The term 'material' here is used in the sense of it being 'significant', and as opposed to 'immaterial'. On the side of the record company, material breach could be defined as the non-payment of royalties or advances due, or that the company has gone into liquidation. On the side of the artist, material breach might be failing to deliver an album due under the agreement.

Whichever side is in material breach, the contract will provide a period – usually 30 days following the notification – within which the breach must be rectified or some other compromise reached. Failing this, whichever side has been in breach risks the other side terminating the agreement.

## (xiv) Miscellaneous Provisions

The recording contract will usually finish up with a few pages of miscellaneous clauses, setting out, for example:

- That the agreement is to be governed by English law;

- That the artist warrants that there are no restrictions which would prevent the artist from entering into the deal (such as being already signed to another record label);

- That nothing in the agreement shall be deemed to create a joint venture or partnership between the artist and the company;

- That the artist acknowledges that the sales of records are speculative and will not sue the company on the basis that more records could have been sold;

- Specifically agreed minor terms, such as the record company agreeing to pay the artist's legal costs in negotiating the agreement – on a recoupable basis, of course.

## (xv) The Signature

The final page of the agreement will provide spaces for signature by the artist and the authorised signatory for the record company. In addition, both sides may be required to initial each page of the agreement to indicate that it is 'read and agreed' – a good practice which removes the possibility of any future dispute over the precise terms of what was signed. That's a polite way of saying that it stops dodgy record companies from inserting new pages into the agreement later.

# Favoured Nations

You may hear the expression 'favoured nations' during your negotiations. If you asked for 'favoured nation' terms, it would mean that you would expect no worse terms than, or as good as, anyone else was being offered. An example might be that you were asked for a licence deal whereby one of your tracks was to appear on a compilation album. Rather than try to ascertain what terms everyone else was being offered, if favoured nations is agreed, you are protected.

# Different Types of Record Deal

The structure set out on the preceding pages covers the standard scenario where a record company is signing an artist directly. Sometimes artists will use what is known as a 'service company' to provide their services to the company, usually for tax reasons. However, in these cases the company will still insist that the artist signs a personal 'inducement letter' which means he will still be signed to the company personally if his service company ceases to provide his services in the future.

There are numerous other types of agreements whereby record companies obtain the rights to exploit artists' recordings. Here are some examples:

## (i) Licence Deals

A licence deal between an artist, or the artist's production company, and a record company usually occurs in one of the following situations:

The artist may have funded the production of recordings himself, and thus owns the copyright and all other rights in them himself. He may not wish to sign personally to the record company and give them options on his future product, or he may wish to do a deal for only a particular territory.

Alternatively, a major artist might have reached the end of his minimum commitment with a company and now be renegotiating a new deal from a position of power. As part of the deal, the company may agree to take future albums on a licence deal for a shorter period of exploitation than under the original contract, and even to add into the deal previous albums made by the artist for the company.

In these situations the artist is known as the 'licensor' and the company is the 'licensee'.

Licence deals still involve the company being granted the right to manufacture, sell and distribute the recordings that are the subject of the deal, and payment to the artist licensor is still usually by way of a royalty. In effect, licence agreements are all about retaining some element of control over distribution and exploitation, as well as – to a lesser extent – areas such as artwork. Artists who are in a position to command licence deals usually receive the benefit of improved royalty rates and smaller packaging deductions, as well as the security of knowing that the rights to their work will be returned to them upon the expiration of the deal.

It is certainly the case that artists, managers or production companies who have funded the recording of a fantastic album themselves will benefit from higher royalties and advances, as recompense for removing a significant amount of risk from the record company. If the company can hear what it is buying upfront, is desperate to sign it and thinks it might need only some fine-tuning or remixing to be a huge album, then the chequebook will be more readily opened.

A sample licence deal for an album can be found in Appendix 11.

## (ii) Profit Split Deals

Independent labels with limited funding are often prepared to be extremely flexible on the terms of their deals with artists. Apart from a formal renegotiation, a major label will not usually vary the terms of its deal, other than by offering an increase in the royalty rate on sales above a certain number of units.

Profit-split deals come in all shapes and sizes but essentially involve the label agreeing to take all of its expenditure 'off the top' of income it receives from record sales. (This expenditure includes normally non-recoupable items, such as marketing and promotion.) The resulting sum is then split with the artist in an agreed percentage.

Some kind of advance against the artist's share of net income will be offered, but this is unlikely to be at a level to get too excited about because, if the label was in a position to offer large advances, it is consequently unlikely that they would need to do a profit-split deal. Undoubtedly, should an artist become extremely successful under the wing of an independent label, a profit-split deal can mean that the net income to the artist is substantially higher than under a standard deal. On the downside, an artist might find that, on a relatively low-selling record, there is an extremely low or non-existent net profit once the costs have been deducted.

## (iii) Deals With Production Companies

Production companies have proliferated in the last decade. Essentially, a production company usually provides none of the services of a record company except the creation and ownership of recordings. It relies instead on licence arrangements with 'real' record companies to release these recordings and to ensure the marketing and distribution of its product. Often, production companies are set up by managers who also wish to take rights ownership in their clients' recordings, or by recording studios who wish to use dead time to generate recordings that might have a rights value. Some production companies style themselves as labels, and may in fact have an exclusive licence deal with a record company that has agreed to release some or all of the production company's product. Others will make great play of their supposed links with a major label, perhaps because they have produced or licensed a hit single with the major recently.

With studio-based production companies, one danger is that the full hourly or daily rate for studio time will be added to the artist's debit balance, and the production company will recoup this. To be cynical, it is in the production company's interests to let the artist use as much time as possible in their studio under these arrangements when, if hard cash was changing hands, cheaper studio deals and shorter sessions would be the order of the day.

Essentially, what it all boils down to is that, if a production company offers you what is effectively a record deal, you can be certain that, as and when the production company licenses the resulting recordings to a 'real' company, you will be receiving less in terms of advances and royalties than if you had signed directly to the record company. This is because the production company is effectively a middle man between you and the record company, making a margin on what it receives and what it pays on to you.

This gives rise to two main problems. First, if the production company is also your manager, he is effectively getting two bites of the cherry: a profit on his licence deals with record companies, and then his management commission on whatever he pays to you. Some might say this is unfair.

Second, what about recoupment? Let's say your production company agrees to pay you an advance of £4,000 for a single. It then licenses the single to a major for an advance of £8,000 and pockets £4,000. When enough singles have been sold to recoup the £4,000 it has paid to you, it is still £4,000 or so unrecouped under its deal with the major, assuming the royalty rates are about the same. Even if the production company is paying you much less in royalties than it receives, it will still be unrecouped. So where is it going to find the money to pay you, now that you have recouped and it hasn't? If the production company is financially stable and has other income, this shouldn't be a problem.

Many production companies don't offer to pay over even a percentage of the advances that they receive from licence deals, offering royalties only. At the end of the day, the copyright in your masters may end up being owned by a production company that has concluded a complex web of licence deals around the world and has then gone bust, owing you substantial royalties on sales which it has not received, as its licence deals are still unrecouped.

It can get even more complicated if the production company has several artists signed to it and has negotiated an overall licence deal for all of its product, receiving an overall advance from its licensee. In this case, there is a danger that the advances will be cross-collateralised across all the product licensed, and if one piece of product sells particularly well and is substantially recouped, the production company might still be unable to pay over the royalties due to its artists. In other words, if you were the successful artist, your royalties might end up being used to cover the losses of the failures.

I would advise any artist offered a deal by a production company to be cautious and let their solicitor ask the tough questions that need to be asked. It is extremely difficult for any artist to turn down a deal on offer, I know, but at the very least you need to be aware of every possible pitfall inherent in putting a middle man between you and a record company.

# The Relationship Between The Artist And The Record Company

It is worth mentioning here that there is a common misunderstanding about the nature of the relationship between an artist and the record company. The artist does not 'work' for the company, in the sense of having a job and being employed by the company, and the advances paid by the company are not 'wages'. Instead, the artist is usually a self-employed individual – a sole trader – or employed through his own service company, perhaps as a director of that company. The record company has simply signed an agreement whereby the artist agrees to render his exclusive services as a recording artist to the company.

Often, in the case of artists signing to smaller labels who are not able to pay reasonable (or any) advances, the artist in question remains in whatever employment he may have had before he was signed, provided that this doesn't put him in breach of any of his obligations under the record deal.

Similarly, artists don't work for managers – it should be the other way around (see Chapter 4) – and only rarely for music publishers (say, as an in-house composer).

49

# Recoupment

There is one aspect to recoupment which may have occurred to you – that is, that the record company begins to 'make money' on a successful record much sooner than the artist. This is because the record company makes a quite substantial margin over and above the artist royalty on each sale.

The artist royalty, and only this, is used to pay back all the recoupable costs. Any non-recoupable costs, such as marketing, the record company's wage bill, rent and so on, are paid for by the record company out of its profit margin.

So, if an artist is £750,000 unrecouped and earning a royalty of £0.75 per album, recoupment would take place at 1 million units sold. If the record company had spent a further £750,000 which was non-recoupable, its total spend would be £1.5 million. Yet its margin on each album (including the artist royalty) should be around £4 per CD. So, £1.5 million divided by £4 means that the record company begins to 'make money' after selling 375,000 CDs, when the artist still has another 625,000 sales to go before reaching the recoupment barrier.

# Conclusion

Record deals are complex, binding legal agreements concerning the exploitation of rights. They have the ability to affect the financial and personal freedom of artists for long periods, and the rights given to record companies within them usually subsist long after the death of the artist.

The signing of a record deal, with any type of record label or production company, thus has far-reaching consequences and should be viewed with equal measures of excitement and caution.

On no account should you sign, or even agree verbally to sign, a record deal without the benefit of advice from a qualified solicitor who specialises in music-business work.

# CHAPTER 2

# RECORD COMPANIES

Probably the best way to begin this chapter is to describe briefly what a record company is and how the various departments function. I have used a major record company as a model. Smaller companies farm out specific functions – such as promotion – to independent companies on a record-by-record basis, or totally, in areas such as Business Affairs, by employing outside solicitors.

There is no such thing as an 'average' major record company, but, to generalise, majors tend to employ between 200 and 400 people in the UK and be based in west or central London, and they are usually owned by an overseas parent company. Majors almost always have personnel based in the regions as A&R scouts and sales reps, but it is fair to say that the 'music business' is almost totally concentrated in London.

Majors also control many smaller labels who they license product from or own, and/or fund. 'Label deals' proliferated in the 1980s, as majors found themselves losing artists to more artist-friendly young companies who had everything going for them except cash. Enter the majors in a blur of chequebooks.

One advantage of major record companies – apart from financial stability – is that they provide an organised structure for an artist's international career. The majors are, at the time of writing, EMI, Universal, Sony/BMG and Warner.

It is important to differentiate between companies and labels. The above companies, and the smaller companies that they own or license, release records under their own name. However, within them they also have a huge number of labels, or 'imprints', under which they release records, and these labels often do not sign acts – for example, Mercury Records (part of Universal) has the

Fontana label within it. Confusingly, record companies are often referred to by the all-inclusive term 'labels'.

Different companies and labels have different cultures, either because they directly specialise in a particular musical genre, such as dance, or because they have built a reputation for breaking a certain type of artist. As examples, the Parlophone label (part of the EMI Group) has a reputation for breaking guitar groups and more heavyweight artists, whereas the EMI label itself has tended to specialise in straight pop acts over the years.

Record companies tend to have departments to cover the following areas of their business, although in some smaller companies departments such as Marketing and A&R are effectively merged.

# The A&R Department

A&R stands for 'Artistes and Repertoire', an historical term dating back to the Tin Pan Alley days of the music business. In those days, A&R people concentrated principally on sourcing the best possible songs for their artists from music publishers. Nowadays, A&R people have two main functions: to spot new talent and ensure that it's signed to their company, and (once the artist is signed) to be the artist's creative contact with the record company. By this I mean that the A&R person will choose songs (either written by the artist or other writers) to be recorded by the artist, prepare recording and touring budgets and get them approved within the company, organise demos, suggest producers, book studios and generally ensure that a single or an album is delivered smoothly to the company. A&R people are thus always up to speed on who the latest and hottest producers, writers and mixers are, and also develop a keen instinct for co-writing opportunities for their artists.

An A&R person therefore has an ongoing relationship with an artist and effectively acts as the artist's 'champion' within the company by ensuring that its sales, marketing and promotion people give the artist as much attention as possible. Often, this can bring the A&R person into conflict with other people in the company who do not share their passion for a particular artist, and who can place them in the difficult position of explaining to the artist or manager that a budget has not been approved or a single has been pulled from the schedule, or – worst of all – that the artist is going to be dropped.

A&R departments tend to be staffed by one or two 'scouts', who listen to demos and investigate new bands, and by A&R managers, who also look after the day-to-day creative activities of signed bands. They in turn are usually surrounded by several secretaries and PAs, who try to maintain some kind of order in the often frenetic atmosphere of a buzzing A&R department. Networking is the secret to A&R, whereby the A&R person maintains constant (and often drug- and alcohol-fuelled) links with key managers, producers, promoters, DJs and even lawyers, any one of whom may put him on the scent of the next big thing.

A&R people are only as good as their last hit, though. A failure to sign hit acts, or not spotting hit acts that then go on to have success with other companies, can mean the end of their career. Conversely, if an A&R person signs an act that goes on to have long-term success lasting many years, he is directly responsible for bringing income of perhaps tens of millions of pounds to the company. For this reason, successful A&R people are rewarded with high salaries and perks, and are often given a small personal royalty on hit acts they sign to give them an incentive.

A&R is a labour-intensive job, which means late nights at gigs and in the studio and an often erratic attendance at the office. Most A&R people live and breathe their jobs and often live life in the fast lane to the same extent as their artists. Indeed, a significant proportion of A&R people have been artists themselves at one stage or another.

Spending large amounts of time dealing with and rejecting hopeful bands and managers can be a soul-destroying experience for A&R people, and unsurprisingly most of them develop a personality that is both thick-skinned and capable of extreme bluntness. It is true to say, unfortunately, that many A&R people are extremely flaky when it comes to organising themselves, and it can be bitterly disappointing for a new artist or manager to be promised that a certain A&R person is 'definitely coming' to the gig, that they are 'just trying to park' and so on, only to have them not show up.

As you can imagine, having the power to offer people record deals also involves being under extreme pressure from all quarters of the business. Once an A&R person has decided that they wish to sign an act (after obtaining the approval from the senior members of the department, assuming that he doesn't have unfettered signing power himself), the offer will be put to the band's representatives by the company's Business Affairs department after discussions between them and A&R concerning the level of deal the band are demanding. This stage of negotiations requires all the A&R person's skill in convincing the artists that they should sign to his company, especially if more than one label is interested in the band, and huge amounts of schmoozing and inducements are often required.

Whereas on the one hand it can be incredibly helpful to have an A&R person who believes in the artist heart and soul and shares their creative vision, the downside is that, if he moves to another company or gets fired, the artist may no longer have a champion within the company and his career may be abruptly curtailed. For this reason, artists who have tremendous negotiating power may be able to insist on a 'key man' clause in their contract which states that, if the A&R man leaves, they can also leave the company (although this is extremely rarely agreed to by record companies). In recent years, many A&R departments have been 'downsized' – which, as most people know, is business-speak for 'sacked'. However, many former A&R people are still retained by their former companies as consultants for specific acts, or are given individual projects to work on. There are a great many veteran A&R people within the industry who still have great connections and who can still get access to the people at the very highest levels of labels. If one of these people takes an interest in you, there is no reason why you might not stand an equal chance of getting a deal as if a regular company A&R person got involved.

# The Marketing Department

This department is responsible for marketing the artist and the artist's product (ie singles, albums, DVDs and so on) to the public. By this, I mean selling as many records as possible. The mainstay of the department is the 'product manager' who is responsible for putting together marketing campaigns for the artist, organising artwork for sleeves, organising press adverts, doing marketing budgets and ensuring that the artist receives adequate press, TV and radio support and efficient distribution into the shops.

In carrying out these functions, Marketing is involved in the styling of the artists, often hiring independent image consultants – stylists – to groom and dress the artists in whatever is deemed the appropriate image for their particular style of music. The right image, the right photo session and the right flyposter can be the calling card that makes the man in the street receptive to a new artist's music, and at this stage half the battle is won.

The department will be involved very early on in the choice of singles and can even have a say in which tracks are actually recorded in the first place, depending on the type of act. There is constant and close liaison between Marketing and A&R throughout the process of bringing the artist's work into the public forum.

Within Marketing are the in-house TV and radio promotions staff, who 'plug' the artist's single or album to TV, and radio producers/researchers and bookers, who secure that elusive video play on MTV or the first Radio 1 single play. Effective plugging is the first traditional stage in any campaign for a new artist or a new release by an established artist, and no stone is left unturned or scam untried in securing exposure for the artist on radio and TV.

Only rarely nowadays are TV and radio producers so desperate to get the exclusive on the latest release from a superstar artist that they will put up with any hassle from the label; in almost all cases, Marketing will go through hoops to secure the right break for whichever artist is deemed to be that week's priority act – for example, paying huge sums to provide satellite links to *Top Of The Pops* from some corner of the globe, or flying presenters and producers out to see shows wherever they want. If plugging is beginning to sound rather like legalised bribery, that's because (with respect) it is!

The Press Office also usually comes under the control of the Marketing department and is responsible for getting records reviewed in the music and other press and getting interviews for artists. It becomes involved almost as soon as product is ready, leaking out advance CDs to key journalists, along with invitations to showcase gigs, gifts and gimmicks, and an endless supply of lunches.

Many independent companies deal in press for bands and/or plugging records to radio and TV. All major labels draw on the expertise of independents from time to time, and in practice very few superstar artists have their records plugged 'in house' by the record company's own staff, preferring instead to build up a relationship with an outside plugger over many years. The plugging companies with the most star clients wield considerable power in the music business.

Whether or not an artist is a 'priority act' is one of the major concerns of Marketing. Because of the large numbers of releases in an average month at a major record label, inevitably some singles and albums are not given the full muscle of the department's attention. Being a priority act means that every relevant department in the company is working all-out to make a record a hit by any means possible, fair or foul.

With new artists, the advent of the Internet and online marketing initiatives have been an incredible boon in establishing early word-of-mouth on an artist, and the artist's own website is a critical tool in this process. Whether it is a case of spamming other band's sites to promote the new band, providing effective links and reviews from other sites, or creating of a 'street team', the importance of these relatively new techniques cannot be overestimated.

# The Business Affairs Department

This department comprises solicitors and other legal executives who concern themselves with negotiating recording contracts with artists' solicitors as well as other contractual matters in the artist's relationship with the company. Business Affairs and A&R work closely together to ensure that the right deal is struck when an artist signs. Once signed, an artist's deal can be altered and added to – for example, if the company agrees to pay tour support (the budget shortfall of a tour), the artist will have to sign a side agreement confirming that the costs will be repaid from his royalties. Business Affairs would draft this document and every other contract concerning the artist.

One of the most important functions of the department is keeping track of how long the artist's contract with the company has to run, and when options are due. If the company wishes to record another album, it must 'exercise its option' by issuing a notice confirming that the artist is entering the next period of their contract and (usually) paying the next contractual advance.

The department also works closely with the company's Finance division to work out the cost implications of picking up an option, and is usually heavily involved in discussions with A&R in deciding whether or not to continue with a particular artist's contract.

Business Affairs will also conclude agreements with producers, engineers and session musicians who are to work with the company's artists, and will usually also negotiate licence agreements with third parties wishing to license the company's recordings – for example, on compilation albums. In addition, the department will usually represent the company at various industry committees within organisations such as the BPI (see later) to ensure that the company's position on the wider legal and contractual issues facing the industry is put forward.

In most major record companies, the Royalties department comes under the auspices of Business Affairs. The function of the Royalties department is to analyse sales data from every territory in which the company's recordings are sold, and on every release, and then to calculate the royalties due to artists, producers, mixers, licensees and other parties, based on the contracts that the company has signed with them. Once this gargantuan task has been undertaken, the department issues the royalty statements that are due to each party, along with any due payments.

# Sales, Distribution And Manufacturing

Sales are usually achieved by a combination of telesales – where shops phone in their orders for records or order online – and reps visiting shops personally to promote the company's latest releases and take orders for them. The reps also carry stock for the shops. Sales forces – teams of reps for different areas of the country – work closely with Marketing, ensuring that product is in the shops to coincide with the press, TV and radio activity that Marketing has generated.

The aim is to distribute records effectively, and there are many totally independent distribution companies who are used by record companies for this function. Unsurprisingly, all sales reps know exactly which record shops are 'chart return' shops – ie those shops whose sales are logged into CIN's (The Chart Information Network's) computers and which provide the figures on which the charts are based. These shops are singled out for special attention and are the first to receive special formats of singles, window displays and even free goods.

In practice, a great many singles are simply given free of charge to the chart shops by reps on the understanding that the shop will sell them at cut price and put them through its CIN machine. (Such logged sales are known as 'panel sales'.) This can ensure a chart entry which, in theory, will draw attention to the single, therefore producing real sales and an eventual hit.

The Sales department is also responsible for many of the activities which tend to be described as 'hyping' – for example, hiring teams of people to go into chart return shops and buy copies of a particular single in the hope of artificially affecting its chart position.

Manufacturing of the company's stock is either carried out at the company's own pressing plants – often centralised across Europe – or subcontracted out to independent manufacturers.

# The International Department

Major record companies form part of multinational conglomerates, and their artists need to succeed internationally before significant profits can be made. America is the golden goose, comprising over 50% of the worldwide record market. Other major markets are the so-called GAS territories (Germany, Austria and Switzerland), Japan and Canada. When a UK major's affiliated company sells a record by an artist signed to the UK company, the affiliate pays the UK company a royalty which, although high, allows the UK company to make a margin before paying the royalty due to its artist. The affiliate keeps the profit margin on top for each sale in its territory and pays the appropriate publishing royalties to the publishers in that territory.

The International division's function is to ensure that the company's affiliates around the world are kept up to date with new available product, and to assist other territories in marketing an artist once they have decided to release their album. This will involve the creation of an international marketing and promotion plan for an artist, often coinciding with a tour, the aim of which will be to have the artist being marketed and promoted in as many countries as possible in as short a timescale as possible. In the case of releases by major artists, the company will present its forthcoming product to its international companies at conferences throughout the year, at which the artists often appear. Thus, if certain territories get particularly excited about a certain artist, the international plan will be weighted towards that territory.

International also ensures that production parts (ie master tapes and artwork files) are serviced to the company's overseas affiliates, along with biographies, videos and other promotional tools. Increasingly, majors have created divisions that span entire continents to handle the international marketing and promotion of their artists.

On the back of a substantial hit in their home territory, a new artist can become a 'international priority' act and have the full machinery of the label at its disposal worldwide. This means that each territory is under strict instructions to break the act in that territory and to sell as many records as possible.

It may seem bizarre to artists coming to the industry anew that their record may not get released outside the UK, particularly as the record company will almost certainly have taken worldwide rights. The truth is that the one problem that record companies do not have is lack of product, and each company in a major territory will potentially be creating dozens of hopeful 'priority' albums during an average year. The upside of this is that there are numerous UK and American artists who, although their album might not have set the cash registers ablaze in their home territory, have sold as substantial numbers of records in, say, Japan and are therefore saved from the 'drop zone' and given the chance to make another record. From the point of view of such artists, this is nothing but good news, not least because, whilst they might struggle to pull 500 people in London, they may be able to play to 5,000 in Tokyo and make a fortune on ticket sales and merchandising.

# PROPORTION OF WORLD SALES BY REGION 2000 - 2003

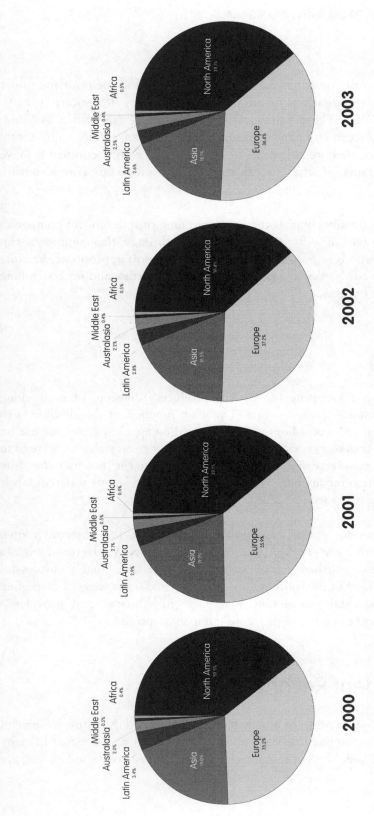

# Video

Some major record companies have a dedicated division for releasing music videos – either compilations of an artist's promo clips or concert specials, primarily via DVD. These videos, which are retailed, are known as 'long-form videos'. Record companies almost always sign an artist's audio-visual rights as part of their record deal. In recent years, record companies have usually amalgamated these dedicated music video divisions within Marketing.

Marketing also usually controls the commissioning of independent companies to produce promo clips for the latest singles, through the company's clip commissioner, who is responsible for suggesting the most appropriate directors and production companies to work with a particular artist, and for controlling the appropriate budgets.

# Licensing

All majors have a Licensing (or 'Special Products') division, often working within the Business Affairs structure. The main function of this division is to license the company's recordings to other record companies, either for use on compilation albums or as entire releases. The recordings may also be licensed to film companies or advertising agencies. An album from the '60s may therefore be owned by one company but, over the years, appear on many different labels as new licensing deals are concluded.

Often, this division is also responsible for releasing the company's own compilations, either low- or mid-price releases or major TV-advertised releases featuring long-established brand names, such as the hugely successful *Now…That's What I Call Music!* series. Licensing and other ways of marketing the majors' old catalogue albums is a huge growth area and provides a substantial contribution to major record companies' profits.

# Independent Record Companies

It is rare to find an example of a truly independent record company, by which I mean a company that has absolutely no links whatsoever with a major. In many cases, seemingly independent companies, with all the cred of an indie label, are actually part-owned by a major, which may have taken the option to buy the independent in full after a certain point.

Other independents are licensed exclusively to certain majors, either worldwide or, more often, outside the UK. The sheer cost and administration required in operating a full-service record label in each major record market of the world is beyond the scope of almost all independent record labels, and so they need to plug into the infrastructure of a major in order to reap at least some success.

It is often said that the independents have effectively acted as the unpaid A&R departments of the majors, taking the risks on the first releases by new artists only to have them snapped up by the majors at the first signs of success. To a large extent, this is true, although there is usually some spin-off benefit for the independents, such as increased back-catalogue sales for albums by that artist which it may still own, or a share of future royalties on albums recorded for the major.

There are upsides and downsides for artists in dealing with independents, which become more extreme the smaller the company is. Upsides include often total commitment to artists, without the pressures of big-company politics and accountants; more flexible deal structures (on occasions involving no contracts at all); and, perhaps, a more open-minded creative approach than that of a major.

The downsides can be acute cash problems, a lack of organisation and structure (particularly relating to an artist's international career) and an over-dependence on one or two strong personalities in the company, who may not be there forever.

## THE STRUCTURE OF A RECORD COMPANY

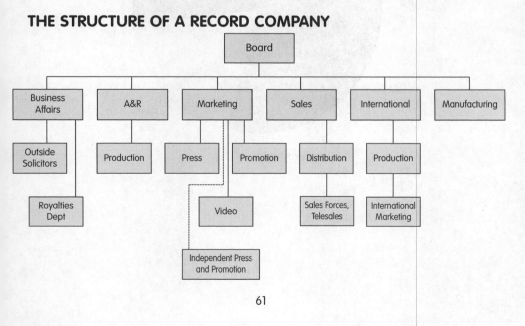

Ultimately, everyone has their price, and independents are always vulnerable to being made an offer they can't refuse by a major. As soon as an independent develops an interesting new artist, the majors will be courting the company, either by making an offer to distribute it or license it in certain territories, or by acquiring a stake in it.

As the artists signed to the independent can be 'sold' as part of it (depending on the terms of their contracts), they are often powerless to keep control of their careers. Having said that, very successful indie artists often get given shares in (or end up owning) the labels they are signed to as an inducement to make them stay, which may be worth a fortune in the event of a buyout.

## RECORD COMPANY MARKET SHARE, ALBUMS 2003

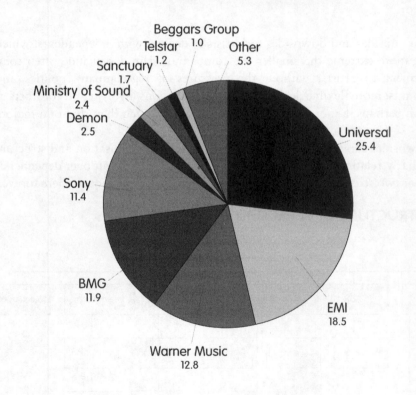

# CHAPTER 3

# MUSIC PUBLISHING AND SONGWRITING

## Introduction

Music publishing is the second major platform of the music industry. Music publishers actively seek new talent in the same way as record companies, as well as working with established writers whom they publish. Again, in the same way that record companies exploit recordings, music publishers exploit songs in order to earn money for themselves and the songwriters who are signed to them.

Although recordings of songs is the medium which generates the vast majority of a music publisher's income, it is important to understand that publishers do not usually have any rights in such recordings, only the actual song which is embodied on the recording. Once again, understanding the difference between a song and a recording of a song is crucial.

Perhaps one way to illustrate this difference is that a recording, even after numerous remixes and edits, remains the same recording by the same artist. Even if parts of it are sampled, that sample is still the same recording, albeit placed within another recording. A song, on the other hand, once written, can in theory be performed, reproduced or recorded by numerous different people at different times, provided that the necessary permissions are obtained and the correct payments are made to the writer or, more usually, his publisher.

Songs are the true foundation stones of the music industry. Although it's an obvious point to make, songs have existed for thousands years longer than the ability to make recordings of them. When most people talk about something being a 'great record', they usually mean 'great song' rather than 'great playing' or 'great production'. Great songs can become timeless classics, rising beyond the limitations of the recording technology used at the time.

If you're a songwriter as well as a potential recording artist, you have the ideal combination of talents. If you're in a band but don't contribute to the songwriting, the blunt truth is that you're unlikely to earn as much as the members of the band who are writers once you get signed, unless the writers agree to split songwriting royalties with you as gesture of good faith.

It is therefore vital that you develop an understanding of how music publishing works, and what legal and financial issues arise from the ownership and exploitation of songs. At first sight, the world of music publishing may seem mystifying, but read on...

# What Is Copyright?

In simple terms, owning or controlling the 'copyright' in a 'work' (a song, a book, a recording and a picture are all examples of so-called 'works') means the right to prevent somebody else copying that work, as well as the right to make people pay for copying and using or exploiting such works. Current UK copyright legislation is embodied in the Copyright, Designs and Patents Act, 1988. The Act states that the owner of the copyright in a work is the person (or company) who first created it, and that the 'maker' of the work is the person who paid for the work to be created or 'arranged' for the work to be created. Thus, record companies tend to own the copyright in the recordings they exploit, because they 'made' them.

Copyright (rather like a new car) does not always remain with the same owner forever. In fact, the sale of copyrights, and the licensing of certain rights in them, is a fundamental part of the music business. When copyrights are transferred to another person or company, they are legally 'assigned'. When only certain rights in the copyrights are granted, and the copyright does not change hands by way of assignment, in most cases such arrangements are by way of a 'licence'.

Let's take a working example. Let's say you are an instrumentalist who has a finished master recording of a dance track. You played all the instruments, wrote the tune, recorded it on hard disk and paid for all the copying, without any help from anyone. You thus own the copyright in both the tune and the recording of it.

A record label comes to you and offers you £1,000 as an advance against a royalty to put the track on a dance compilation album, and you agree. You sign a licence agreement with the label, giving them the right to use the track on the album for an agreed period, provided that they pay you the agreed royalty. You still own the copyright in the recording, as you have only licensed certain rights to them.

The label also has to seek your permission as the owner/writer of the tune for a so-called 'mechanical licence' (see later), whereby the label is permitted to copy the tune every time a copy of the album is pressed.

Take an alternative scenario. You are completely skint, and the label wants to buy the track and the tune from you and own all the rights themselves. They are prepared to pay you a flat fee of £1,000, but no further royalties. In this case, you would be required to assign the copyright in the recording and tune to the label, and you would no longer own either of them. The label could do what it liked with them without any further reference to you. Effectively you would have sold the rights to them in the same way as you might sell a car to someone.

As we have seen in the context of a record deal, ownership and control of copyrights is the very lifeblood of the industry. When you sign a record deal, you are granting the record company the right to create copyrights which embody your performances. A publishing deal grants to the publisher, by way of assignment, copyrights which you originally own and create.

# How To Protect The Copyright In Your Songs

Let's imagine that you've just recorded your first ever demo, containing four original songs, all of which were written by you. You're just about to send hundreds of CDRs off to the far corners of the music business. How do you protect yourself from some unscrupulous person ripping off one of your songs and claiming to have written it himself?

The short answer is that you can't. All you can do is make sure that you have the ability to prove that you owned the copyright in the songs as at a certain date, so that you may be able to sue whoever has infringed your copyright. There are many methods of helping to prove this.

Firstly, always write the following information on the CDR and the packaging:

> 'All songs written by [name]. © [year] [name]. All songs are copyright control. The copyright in these sound recordings is owned by [name]. All rights reserved.'

A bit long-winded I know, but necessary. See later for other CDR packaging tips.

Next, place one CDR in a Jiffy bag. Seal the bag with wax, if you can. Address it to yourself and write the names of the songs on the outside of the bag, then post it to yourself by registered post, keeping the registered post slip. When it arrives, keep it in a safe place.

Alternatively, you can deposit your CDR with a solicitor after swearing an affidavit that the works are your copyright. Or, if you have a family member who is a recognised professional such as a solicitor, doctor or accountant, deposit a copy with them and obtain a dated receipt setting out the song titles on their headed paper.

This probably all sounds a bit tedious, so the following story will illustrate why it's necessary. A mate of mine, when he was in a school band, entered a 'Battle Of The Bands'-type contest where the winning bands were picked from cassette by a panel of judges. One of the judges was in a reasonably well-known chart band at the time. Years later, my mate heard a song on that band's next album which was clearly a total rip-off of his song, yet there was no way of proving that they had entered the song into the competition, when the song was written and who wrote it.

# Publishing Companies

Like record companies, major publishing companies in the UK tend to be based in London. The major publishers also tend to be owned by the same corporate groups that own the major record labels. In addition, there is a healthy independent section of companies that tend to be smaller operations than the majors, as well as myriad small publishers which are no more than an extension of a small record label and tend to publish only artists signed to that record label.

Publishing is administratively intensive, with much more emphasis than a record company on the 'back room'. A publisher can control and exploit the same song for decades, and often for the entire life of the copyright in that song. Publishers, aside from scouting for new talent (particularly if a new artist is getting serious interest from record labels), spend their time policing the use of their copyrights and collecting the income due, either themselves or by using a collecting society such as the MCPS (see later), followed by accounting to their writers. With the advent of digital exploitation of music, the administration of music publishing rights on a global scale is incredibly complex, and it can take several years for any income that has been generated in a particular territory finally to trickle down to the publishers and writers to whom it is due.

Publishers also sign writers who are not themselves recording artists, although it is fair to say that a large number of these kind of signings are of established writers who were maybe once artists themselves, and have a track record of writing hits. Another example would be where a writer, although not himself an artist, is co-writing with a recording artist. In the main, publishers are looking to sign writers who are also artists, as this increases the likelihood of usage of the songs written by the writer.

A criticism frequently levelled at publishers is that they don't do enough artist development and simply act as a kind of passive bank, creaming off money for nothing as and when a band becomes successful. This is not entirely fair. Publishers do work with record labels at the initial stages of a band's career, and are sometimes the first to demo bands, make creative suggestions and occasionally offer to fund touring or a low-budget single release. Later in the band's career, the band's publisher will liaise closely with the record company's A&R department to ensure that the right songs are chosen for an album project, or that the right collaborators are suggested, right through to placing the writer's music in movies and adverts.

In addition, the A&R role of publishers encompasses attempting to obtain cover versions of their writers' songs – in other words, 'pitching' songs to managers, record company A&R men, producers and artists by suggesting that a particular artist records (or 'covers') that song. It is also true to say that, in general, publishers have been better than record labels at operating as a collective industry force, and more adept at ensuring that rates of payment for usages have been agreed quickly so that income has continued to flow to them and their writers.

# What Do Music Publishers Do?

The business of music publishing can be summed up as follows:

(a)     The origination or acquisition of new copyrights as songs or instrumental pieces;

(b)     Licensing or otherwise granting permission to users to use such copyrights;

(c)     Promoting and exploiting such copyrights to generate income;

(d)     Collecting and distributing the income arising from usage of their copyrights;

(e)     Protecting the publisher's copyrights by suing those who infringe them; and

(f)     Generally, finding and nurturing talented songwriters and composers.

# The Terms Of A Music Publishing Contract

This is where the going gets tough, but it is important to understand the details of publishing contracts in order to appreciate how a song is used by publishers, and what share of the income is due to the writers.

The main terms of a publishing contract will specify:

## (a) How many songs the writer is required to deliver to the publisher, during what period, and that the writer is signed exclusively to the publisher

Rather like the Minimum Commitment to be found in a record deal, this clause is designed to set out the number of works to be delivered by the writer to the publisher, and during what period. The number of works to be delivered for an artist/writer is usually tied to specific product, such as an album containing, say, 12 works, not less than 80% of which are written by the writer.

The Initial Period under a standard deal is likely to be one year, which will be extended by the publisher if the Minimum Commitment has not been delivered, or recorded, or released, depending on the specific wording of the agreement. Most publishers will insist that a particular song can fulfil the Minimum Commitment only if it has been released by a major record label in a major territory. In other words, your song could be Number One in Latvia for three months and it wouldn't count towards fulfilment of your Minimum

Commitment, regardless of how much it earned you or the publisher. The Initial Period may, in effect, last for three or even four years if it requires extending because of non-fulfilment of the Minimum Commitment.

From the publisher's perspective, the copyrights they have paid for will not begin earning any income until they are exploited, and it is understandable that the publisher will expect the security of extensions if the Minimum Commitment has not been delivered.

Most publishers will also want the rights to songs written before the commencement of the agreement (unless these songs have already been assigned to another publisher) and also to songs whose composition begins before, but are completed during, the term of the agreement.

If a publisher signs a writer who is not an artist, the Minimum Commitment will almost certainly be that the writer has to have between three and six songs commercially released in each contract period. Parts of songs also count, so if a writer writes 50% of six songs which are released, effectively they have written the equivalent of three whole songs.

## (b) That the publisher is entitled to extend the contract for further periods by way of option

Again, like a record deal, the publisher will want to have further contract periods and further Minimum Commitments during such periods, at their exclusive option. A standard publishing agreement may ask for three or more options of one further year each (subject to extensions), and in cases where a writer is signed to the publishing arm of his record company, the options may mirror those in the record deal and terminate at the same time (ie be 'co-terminus').

## (c) For how long the publisher will be able to exploit the songs delivered under the agreement, and in what territories

The rights period of exploitation in publishing agreements varies markedly from that in record agreements, when, as we have seen, the record company expects to exploit the recordings created for the entire life of their copyright. Publishers would, ideally, like a rights period (or 'Retention Period') for life of copyright, but they are less likely to be able to negotiate it. A period of between 10 and 15 years starting from the end of the agreement is more usual, with some highly successful artist/writers being able to negotiate a much shorter period. It goes without saying that, from the writer's point of view, the shorter the period, the better, as at the end of the period the copyrights are returned to the writer, who may then be able to assign them to a new publisher for a new advance.

The publisher may try to differentiate between those works performed by the writer as an artist and those that are cover versions in negotiating the Retention Period, arguing that the Retention Period in respect of covers should be longer in recognition of the work done by the publisher in obtaining the cover version in the first place. However, this argument is weakened by the publisher usually having negotiated a higher split of income in its favour with the writer for cover versions. For example, despite the fact that you may be an artist yourself, if your publisher clearly secures a cover version of one of your songs by another artist then, instead of earning, say, 75% at source, you will earn maybe 60% or 65%.

The Retention Period for songs delivered to the publisher which, for whatever reason, the publisher has not exploited, is likely to be less. In these cases, the writer is usually required to serve notice on the publisher that these copyrights have not been exploited (perhaps two years after the deal has ended) and give the publisher a period of, say, three months to exploit them, failing which these particular copyrights will be returned to the writer.

The practical effect of this would be that if, for example, a writer was signed to EMI Music Publishing for several years and delivered many songs to them during that time, those songs would remain published by EMI for the Retention Period under that deal, even if the writer then went on to sign to Sony Music Publishing after the end of their EMI deal and Sony began to publish their new songs.

Publishers will want to publish the works for the world, or for as many territories as are available. Here, assuming that there is any scope for negotiation, the issue is whether it would be better to negotiate deals for each territory with a separate publisher, or even to set up the writer's own publishing operation in certain territories. In almost all cases the decision boils down to money, and the basis on which the writer's royalties are calculated for territories in which the publisher operates through a sub-publisher.

## (d) What royalties the publisher will pay to the writer and on what basis these royalties are calculated – either a percentage of the publisher's net receipts or a so-called 'at source' deal

Publishing royalties are calculated on the basis of either the publisher's gross income or the net receipts received by the publisher in the UK. Outside the UK, most publishing companies will agree that royalties are to be calculated on an 'at source' basis – in other words, even if the publisher uses a sub-publisher to collect its income in a particular territory, royalties are still collected on the basis of the gross income in that territory. If a publisher insists on a 'net receipts' deal, a writer must try to limit the percentage charged by the publisher's sub-publisher, as the higher it is, the lower the net will be. A top limit of 15% of gross income to be charged by the sub-publisher is usually accepted.

If the publisher will agree to pay only on the actual net receipts received by the publisher in the UK, then, as stated above, it is usually possible to agree that the percentage of the gross retained by any sub-publishers will be capped at a reasonable level. Without this, the pot of income in which the writer will be sharing may be significantly reduced by the time it reaches the UK.

It is fair to say that the percentage of royalties payable to writers tends to be between 60% and 80% of gross income, with 70% or 75% being average. In respect of performance income, it will usually be agreed that these percentages will still apply on the publisher's share of performance income, with the writer usually receiving 50% of gross performance income direct from the PRS (see later), if he is a member.

The writer is likely to receive less (and the publisher more) in the case of cover versions (ie songs recorded by someone other than the writer), but any reduction should not apply if the writer is the producer of the cover recording – the logic for this being that the publisher may not have had as much to do with getting the song covered as in the ordinary course of pitching.

Royalties are usually payable to the writer by the publisher twice yearly, within 90 days of the end of each calendar half year, and based on amounts actually received by or credited to the publisher. Publishers provide detailed royalty statements setting out the usage of each of the writer's copyrights that they control and the income generated. In many cases where the writer is also a recording artist, the difference between the sales listed on his publishing statement and those on his record-company statement, cross-referenced with the latest PRS statement, can be quite significant, and it is vital that all writers and managers examine these statements in detail.

## (e) What advances the publisher will pay against these royalties, and in what instalments

Advances under a publishing deal are paid in instalments and reflect both delivery and release of product, rather like a record deal, but also other alternatives. For example, a publisher may expect that the instalments should be linked to signature of the publishing deal, with further instalments being payable when the writer signs a major record deal (here, the publisher is likely to specify precisely which record companies constitute 'majors'), delivery of an album, release of the album, and perhaps even specific chart positions of albums and singles.

The definition of what constitutes an acceptable record deal to the publisher is an area of regular dispute. With so many small 'independent' record labels having links with majors, and so many larger independents having significant commercial success, it is no longer acceptable to simply list the 'Big Four' (EMI, Sony/BMG, Warner and Universal) and refuse to pay up if the writer signs with an alternative label. The publishing deal should therefore reflect this and provide that the publisher must act in reasonable good faith in its definition of a major.

Clearly, the level of these advances will reflect whether the writer is a completely unknown quantity, or is an artist who has already signed a record deal, or has already had hit singles. In the latter case, when the publisher knows that there is income waiting to be collected, advances can be substantial, especially as the writer is likely to have been the subject of a bidding war between rival publishers. Artists who are unpublished writers and are enjoying a hit debut album or single are in an enviable position, and may be able to command advances of hundreds of thousands of pounds on signature of the publishing deal.

It is very common for managers and lawyers without an urgent need for funds to 'wait to do the publishing', as with an album that is selling strongly, or a series of massive hit singles, many potential publishers will be as optimistic about the future as possible and make incredibly high offers.

## (f) That the writer grants to the publisher a full assignment of the copyright in the songs which are the subject of the agreement and waives his moral rights

As previously mentioned, the foundation of any publishing deal is that the writer assigns the copyright in his songs to the publisher. As well as this, the so-called 'moral right', or author's right, specified in the 1988 Act is waived by the writer, allowing the publisher to exploit the copyrights delivered freely. However, the writer may be able to negotiate a provision preventing the publisher from exploiting any version of the writer's work which is materially and detrimentally changed – for example the addition of parodic or derogatory lyrics to the original tune. In addition, if the writers is also an artist, the writer will be able to insist that the publisher grants the 'first mechanical licence' to record the song to him as an artist before anyone else can cover the song.

## (g) The obligations of the publisher

Rather like a record company, the publisher will try to keep its contractual obligation to do anything at all to the absolute minimum. However, it will agree vague wording along the lines that it will use its reasonable endeavours to exploit the copyrights delivered by the writer. It may also agree to provide demo facilities for use by the writer, or the purchase of home studio equipment, although it will require any such expenses to be recoupable. The publisher should also be obliged to register the works delivered under the agreement with the various collecting societies worldwide in order to ensure the efficient collection of income and also the protection of the copyrights. Although any such commitments are unlikely to be contractual, some publishers will agree to contribute to tour support and larger equipment costs on a recoupable basis.

# Where The Record Label Or The Manager Is Also The Publisher

This section is a particular soapbox of mine.

All major music conglomerates worldwide have publishing operations as well as record labels. Generally speaking, they tend to operate autonomously and deal with each other on a reasonably arms-length commercial basis. Indeed, disputes between record companies and publishers (or collecting societies acting for publishers) are fairly regular occurrences, despite there being a certain element of 'Monopoly money' about the financial implications of the areas under dispute.

The possible danger for writers comes in signing to a publisher which is simply a backwater of the record label (or manager) to which the writer is signing as an artist. This can cause problems for a number of reasons. The record label or manager may be refusing to sign the artist unless he also gives them his publishing, and may be in the worst cases attempting to cross-collateralise recording and publishing expenditure. Whilst it is easy to understand the label's or manager's desire to protect their investment by obtaining whatever security they can (the artist's publishing or sometimes even merchandising rights), this practice cannot lead to the best commercial result for the writer. It is, in the worst cases, effectively blackmail based on a clear conflict of interest, as it prevents the writer from seeking alternative sources of income outside the label or manager he is signed to (from another publisher) and means that the writer could be tied to the same people long after his record deal or management deal has gone sour.

Among the key questions the writer must ask himself is whether the 'publisher' is actually a publisher in the accepted sense of the word or just an extension of the record label or management. Will the publisher protect and exploit the copyrights which are to be delivered in any meaningful sense? Also, will the publisher develop the writer's career as a writer by, for example, arranging co-writing sessions and pitching songs? If the publisher then signs a sub-publishing deal with a 'real' publisher after the writer has had some success as a recording artist, will this reduce the writer's share of income to an unacceptable degree? Will the writer get any share of the advance under such a deal? In general, is the 'publisher' properly administered on a worldwide basis?

Often, such deals are pitched to artists and writers as being tremendously advantageous to their careers, using the line that, if anyone such as a major Hollywood studio wants to use a track in a movie, then it's a 'one-stop shop' for them, because a deal for both the recording and the song can be done at the same time. Hmmm. Raise one, or both, eyebrows at this point.

All I can advise is that such arrangements must be treated with extreme caution by a writer, with the assistance of an expert, commercially minded music-business solicitor, who should be able to negotiate an escape route from such a deal if things go wrong. At the risk of repeating myself, try not to sign your publishing to someone or some company that is not actually a publisher.

# Becoming A Professional Songwriter

Most artists with a long-term recording career tend to write their own songs, but many do not. Pop artists, in particular, call on the services of professional songwriters to send them existing demos of the kinds of songs they are after (ie hit songs!) or to write something especially for them. Many respected artist/writers, such as Coldplay's Chris Martin, also write songs for other artists. Equally, former recording artists such as Cathy Dennis have developed hugely successful careers as songwriters for other people.

Unless you are an artist and able to generate attention from the industry using the traditional routes of a great demo, gigs and press, it is extremely difficult to establish yourself as a professional songwriter without years of perseverance and a few strokes of luck.

But let's start with the basics. If you believe that you have a talent for writing songs, then it goes without saying that you will have been writing songs prolifically from an early age and it is almost inconceivable that you will not have some vocal talent, an ability with some kind of instrument, or perhaps skill as a lyricist or programmer. Few professional songwriters began their career without being able to tick at least one of the above boxes. In fact, when asked for some basic advice on becoming a professional songwriter, one young up-and-coming writer put it perhaps best of all: 'Just write lots and lots of songs!'

Most people start writing songs at the piano or on guitar and make basic demos either with and old-fashioned 4-track set up or using a computer, then playing them to friends and family. In reality, unless the budding songwriter has a great voice, these early steps aren't likely to have music publishers breaking their door down. So the first step is to examine what is needed to create great song demos.

Many writers readily accept that they are not the greatest singers in the world and do not have the vocal ability to really 'sell' a song. They therefore use session singers or friends with great voices to record the vocals of their songs. However, in the 21st century, it is fair to say that there are few serious songwriters who do not have a working knowledge of programming and who cannot create instrumental tracks using the huge variety of software available.

Most working writers have a home setup using either Logic, Cubase or Pro Tools, which give them the ability to work for minimal cost to an extremely high standard. Incidentally, numerous hit records have been created using some of the original parts from the songwriter's original demo of the song.

Therefore, the first stage must be to put yourself in a position – with equipment and perhaps a vocalist – where great demos of great songs can be created. If money is an issue, there are numerous ways that a resourceful, budding songwriter can access community or college facilities with which to begin writing and programming.

The second stage is to think about the process by which hit songs are written. You will have noticed that it is unusual for songs to just have one writer. Indeed, numerous hits seem to have at least four writers, although this is often more to do with politics and splitting income than actual creative input.

But the point is that co-writing is probably the best way to move ahead as a songwriter. But co-write with whom?

There must be musicians and bands that you like and respect in your community, or studio engineers and programmers who are also writers, so try doing some co-writing with one of these people. It's a bit nerve-racking at first, but hopefully you will find like-minded musicians and writers with whom you can build a creative bond. If, for example, the engineer at your local studio has been working with a brilliant singer who doesn't write songs, they may have been recording the usual standard songs that everyone records. Try to write something new for them, maybe co-writing with the engineer, and see what they think. If they are a truly great singer and stand a chance of getting a record deal, this can be a fast track to finding yourself a publishing deal.

It goes without saying that if – through whatever means – you can end up co-writing with either a writer who has already got a publishing deal, or an artist who has got a record deal, then your chances of being signed to a publishing deal are vastly improved. Even if you write something with a jobbing songwriter who still has a publisher but hasn't had a hit for years, if it's a great song then their publisher will sit up and take notice of you.

Some songwriters have a particular talent for writing lyrics, which is an area in which many professional songwriters have difficulty. Again, if a local writer is coming up with great backing tracks, maybe you'll find that your strength lies in writing lyrics or 'top lines' (melody lines).

Another increasingly common method by which writers to draw attention to themselves – if they are also performers – is to play at the numerous 'songwriter' evenings held at venues across the country, although mainly in London.

There's no doubt that a certain percentage of the people who think that they can write songs have little or no discernible talent for it. However, rather like playing an instrument or reading music, it is possible to 'learn' songwriting by taking a course and understanding song structure, harmony and what makes a great song. There is no upper age limit to being a great songwriter, and many would suggest that the ability to write great songs improves with age.

One of the most commonly asked questions is, 'Do you need to know how to read music?', and the answer is, 'No.' Many hugely successful songwriters – and, indeed, artists – wouldn't have the first clue how to read or write music, although at the very least all songwriters tend to know roughly what chords they are playing!

# Approaching Publishing Companies

There is no substantial difference in the methods you should use to draw yourself to the attention of publishers to those suggested in Chapter 5 for record companies. Publishers have A&R departments (with their A&R men sometimes given the more archaic name 'professional managers') which are actively seeking new artists, as well as pure songwriters with whom they feel they can do some business. One great advantage of approaching publishing companies – unlike record companies – is that, if some very strong songs are co-written with a published writer, their publisher will not only hear them straight away but will see the merit of picking up the new writer so that the publisher controls the whole song.

As with record companies, certain publishers have developed a reputation in certain areas of music, and rather than waste valuable CDRs and postage you should do some research on which publishers and A&R people seem to favour your particular musical style. There are no rigid rules here, but just as a thrash-metal band shouldn't send a demo to a record label specialising in reggae, the same demo is unlikely to find favour with a country music specialist publisher.

If you are an unproven writer who is never likely to be a performer, then the deals on offer from even the largest major publishers tend not to be hugely lucrative, in terms of advances, but may enable you to become a full-time songwriter. You may have a song that the publisher feels immediately that he will be able to pitch at a major artist, perhaps one with whose manager or record company A&R man he has a strong relationship. Alternatively, you may have been co-writing with an established writer or performer and therefore have a strong likelihood of generating some income for the publisher as soon as the songs are recorded.

There are certain managers who specialise in managing songwriters and record producers (who are often, incidentally, one and the same) rather than traditional artists, and if you can attract their attention they will be able to fast-track you into co-writing on projects for which their other clients are already producing or writing.

Being a professional songwriter is extremely competitive, with numerous writers vying to have their songs pitched to every project or to write something to order. Even the most successful writers are usually still receptive to co-writing with newer artists who either have just got a record deal or who are attracting a certain amount of interest, as writers tend to have periods when they are 'hot' and everyone wants to work with them, and then periods where they are out of favour.

Often, songs can be delivered to a publisher and be pitched around to various projects for a couple of weeks and not get any takers, only for them to be picked up by a major artist years later and earn a fortune. Truly great songs tend to get cut, though, in the end.

# Joining The PRS

Provided that you fulfil the basic membership requirements (see www.prs.co.uk), you need to join the PRS in order to ensure that you're receiving your share of public-performance and broadcast money for your songs. The PRS provides the opportunity to register your songs on their database and, by virtue of their worldwide network of affiliated collection societies, you will begin to see income for a myriad of usages if your songs start to be played or performed.

As a new writer, it may seem far-fetched to imagine that somehow money will trickle down to you from performances and broadcasts of your music (and incidentally, you will almost always get one-half of your performance income directly from the PRS, whatever arrangements you have with a publisher), but the system works. The main thing is to join and to begin registering your songs.

Your PRS statement, which is sent every three months, will make fascinating reading if you're even a moderately successful writer, and it may contain details of everything from BBC Radio plays to background music used in a TV documentary in Uruguay.

# Songwriting Splits

This is a difficult area in which to suggest any hard-and-fast rules, probably for the same reasons that made me reject the idea of a chapter called something like 'How To Form A Band' – there is no right answer, and unfortunately almost anything is going to sound vague.

But, for the sake of argument, let's say that you're in a four-piece band and you're all songwriters. You probably all come to rehearsals with either a few ideas for a song or one that is almost fully written, so some songs will clearly be the brainchild of one member of the band more than others. In these cases, maybe 75% of the song should be allocated to that member, with the remaining 25% split between the other three. If a complete song is brought in, but with no lyrics, then whoever writes the lyrics might expect to be credited with writing half of the song.

You might decide that, as all the band contribute to the 'arrangement' of each song, 20% of each song is always split equally between all the band (5% each), come what may.

In the case of professional songwriters going into a room together, it's almost certainly the case that any song written would be split equally, regardless of the fact that one of them might have written most of the lyrics and another one might have spent most of the session on the phone.

Ultimately, unless you decide to just split everything equally – which can lead to massive problems later if the main songwriter begins to resent giving away so much of his income – it's a matter of even-handed negotiation and compromise. Hopefully, if you become a successful artist, you'll avoid the nightmare scenario of substandard songs having to appear on your albums simply so that certain members of the band feel they're getting their rightful slice of the publishing pie.

Once you've agreed the split on each song, it's vital to write this down in some form and have each member of the band sign the document, indicating their agreement. At least then in the future, if one member of the band gets a deal and begins using the songs so that they generate publishing income, the other members of the band are protected and will receive their share.

A brief trawl of the Internet and an examination of the well-known legal disputes concerning Spandau Ballet, and also The Smiths, will provide the best possible argument for sorting out songwriting splits sooner rather than later.

# How Much Do Songwriters Earn?

Most music publishers would probably mutter, 'Far too much,' and the reality is that percentage splits are weighted in favour of the writers, and have been for decades. It is actually fairly straightforward to calculate roughly how much a writer will earn if one knows the sales levels of albums which have the writers songs on them, because mechanical royalties are based on known percentages of known prices and, in the USA, are based on an actual 'cent rate' for every album sold.

Songwriters earn money, whether via their publisher or directly, through the following main channels:

- Mechanical Royalties – These are sums paid by companies who manufacture records or DVDs. These royalties (in the UK) are usually collected by the MCPS (Mechanical Copyright Protection Society) at the agreed rate (8.5% of dealer price) and then paid through to MCPS members (publishers), minus a small percentage for the MCPS. Rather than go into inordinate detail, most people in the industry use a very rough average that the 'publishing' on a full-price album is worth about 65p. So, on a 75% split, the writer's share of that is just under 50p per copy. In the US, it would work out – and this is very rough – at about 40p a copy at current exchange rates on a 12-track album. So, call the average 45p. If an album sells 2 million copies around the world, using a reasonable mix of territories, the writers should be earning around £900,000 once all the mechanical royalties have been collected.

- Performance Income – These are sums paid mainly either by broadcasters, or by venue owners for the use of songs, calculated at a bewildering array of tariffs by (in the UK) the PRS and then paid through to its publisher and writer members. If the album described above includes three big hit singles that get on the radio all over the world, and there is a European arena tour to sellout crowds, then performance income should at least double the mechanical income, half of which should come directly to the writers from performing rights societies.

- Synchronisation Income – These are sums paid, for example, by film companies and advertisers to 'synchronise' songs (ie put them together with moving images). They are open to negotiation, although some publishers have set 'per minute' rates as a minimum. For a worldwide TV advertising campaign for a computer game, for example, a publisher could expect a fee in the hundreds of thousands of dollars for the use of 30 seconds of a major song. The publisher would pay between 60% and 70% of this to the writer.

- Print Income – Many years ago, print income was a substantial source of income for songwriters, as people would buy sheet music for the piano or guitar to learn how to play the latest hits of the day. Even today, big hit songs can still generate a demand for sheet music, and successful artist/writers still release bestselling songbooks of their music.

As food for thought, even a song that was a substantial hit in the UK 15 years ago and still regularly gets played on the radio and used on compilation albums should still be netting its writers over £10,000 per year, every year. And when it might have taken only 20 minutes to write, that's not bad!

# CHAPTER 4

# MANAGERS

## What Is A Manager?

A manager is a vital factor in obtaining a record or publishing deal, or at least in obtaining one quicker than you can on your own. Once an artist is signed, management can make or break a career. It is probably true to say that any new artist is going to find it more difficult to get a deal of any kind without a manager, simply because industry people feel reassured that somebody is already taking a leap of faith and working with the artist.

Essentially, managers work for artists and are responsible for developing, advancing and strategising the artist's career. Once signed, an artist's relationship with their record company will be conducted almost entirely through the manager, although the artist will get to know many people at the company on a day-to-day level.

The manager will also handle the artist's relationship with their live agent (see later), merchandiser, website people, accountants and lawyers on a day-to-day basis. In addition, the manager will deal with the music publishing issues of artists who are also songwriters. The philosophy behind this structure is that the artist is a creative individual and therefore needs an experienced, trusted person at the helm to ensure that the business aspects of their career are being handled efficiently and that the maximum income is being generated.

In effect, the manager often becomes the artist's alter ego.

There is a school of thought that says you're either a manager or you're not. In other words, you're born a manager. I go along with this to a certain extent. There comes a point when, whatever in-depth knowledge somebody has, the 'inner manager' takes over and they can make a deal or sort out a problem with a unique combination of ego, persuasiveness, lateral thinking and bull-headed belief in their clients, which has characterised all the great managers in the business. If you talk to great managers, you will often find that they were the kind of people at school who organised things, saw different ways to look at problems and relished being the (supposedly) back-room person who in reality ran everything.

A good manager is a tremendous advantage – and, by the same token, a poor manager can ruin an artist's career. The selection of a manager and the contract signed with that manager is therefore one of the most important steps in an artist's career.

Your potential manager need not necessarily be someone who you end up being good mates with, or even someone you necessarily want to have a pint with; the underlying issues are their skills as a manager and whether or not you feel that you can trust him to handle your career (and, in certain circumstances, your money). As the manager will often be the person presenting the views and work of the artist to the industry at large, and will be the first port of call for those interested in a new band, you need to ensure that your manager is creatively in tune with you.

After a period of working together, the best managers develop a sixth sense for what their artist is or is not going to be happy with, which speeds up the communication process and forms the basis of any good working relationship.

Managers make their living by charging a percentage of the artist's earnings. This percentage is known as the manager's 'commission' and is traditionally between 15% and 20% of the artist's gross earnings. It is also normal for the manager to expect the artist to pay certain expenses on top of this, which the manager will incur as part of his day-to-day work managing the artist.

It is worth remembering that some of the world's most successful artists have been with the same managers for decades – true partnerships where both artist and manager have earned substantial incomes.

# Different Kinds Of Manager

Managers can perhaps be grouped into a number of very general categories:

## (i) The Professional Manager

This type of manager will be making his living solely from artist management. It is therefore very likely that he will have one or more clients already signed to a major record label and will have in-depth experience of dealing with record companies. More often than not, he will be based in London, and, depending on how successful he is, may have an office and staff. Occasionally, he will have other financial interests, such as being a promoter at a small gig or having his own small record label or production company.

As a general rule, if a professional manager is interested in a new artist, it is because he believes that the artist stands a good chance of getting a record (or publishing) deal and for him to earn some commission. The very best professional managers will have widespread contacts within the industry and be able to generate interest from A&R people simply on the basis that they are managing a particular artist. Once a manager has a track record of managing hit acts that have gone on to enjoy future long-term success, every record company and publisher will take a strong interest in whoever his new clients are.

There are numerous large artist management companies comprising groups of managers working together. In these cases, the management company itself is usually hired by the artist, with a personal manager working with the artist on a day-to-day basis and, in many cases, being given a personal share of the company's commission, over and above the basic salary that the company pays to the manager.

In the case of an artist being managed by a company, after an approach from one of the company's management staff, it is worth reiterating here the point made in the chapter on record companies about 'key man clauses'. In other words, you may be able to negotiate an escape route from being managed by that particular company if your 'key man' decides to leave or is fired.

There are advantages in being managed by a large, well-established company with a roster of successful clients. The company will have respect and bargaining power within the industry and may be able to create opportunities for its artists to work together – for example, by ensuring that its new artists get the chance to tour in support of its more established clients.

## (ii) The Old Pro

An 'old pro' (my expression) is a manager who perhaps formerly managed one or more successful artists but who now does not have any clients signed to major labels, or indeed signed at all. Perhaps he is semi-retired and in other employment but keeps up his contacts with the music business.

Often, old pros have personal relationships with some of the most senior and influential people in the music business, people who the old pro dealt with at a junior level in his heyday. The old pro will make a very big deal out of these contacts, usually by implying that it will be no problem to get the Managing Director of a major label down to a gig and, by implication, get a deal offer on the table. Whether or not you should be managed by an old pro comes down to how credible you think he or she is – or whether you suspect that you're just being used to help the old pro relive former glories.

There is also a netherworld of 'managers' who are on the periphery of the industry and have little or no direct experience of artist management. They could be, for example, concert promoters, or the more 'cabaret'-orientated agents, or music journalists. To a man (or woman), they all believe that artist management is as easy as falling off a log and will imply that getting a deal, gigs, press and suchlike will be no problem whatsoever. I would urge caution in dealing with such characters; you need to ensure that you are being represented by someone who is not only credible but a realist, too.

Remember also that, as the modern music business is still less than 50 years old, plenty of people who were around in the early days are still on the scene today – and some of them are undoubtedly of questionable ability and credibility.

## (iii) The Enthusiastic Amateur

This is usually a person whose ambition is to become a professional manager, or to get a job in the music business. He or she may be, for example, a college booker or promoter, a roadie or soundman, or just a person with an everyday job who is seduced by the supposed glamour of the music business. Often, the enthusiastic amateur will be a failed musician who realises that, as he's never going to be good enough to play in a band, he can at least manage one.

Often, the great strength of these people is that they can be single-mindedly determined to promote their artist to the point of obsession. They may lack finesse and a proper understanding of the music business, but they do want to learn. Everybody has to start somewhere, and naivety is no worse than being very set in your ways, as some professional managers (and old pros) are.

If you decide to let the enthusiastic amateur have a go at managing you, proceed cautiously and be realistic about how much time he is actually going to be able to give you; he may, for example, have a full-time job, which brings as many advantages (free phone calls!) as disadvantages (lack of time). As long as you feel that he or she will present themselves professionally to the industry and have the drive and ambition to move your career forward, it may be a worthwhile move.

Enthusiastic amateurs are usually short of money but would sell their granny for the good of the artist. As long as you follow the advice in this book regarding management contracts (particularly contract clauses that enable you to walk away from the deal if things aren't happening), being managed by an enthusiastic amateur is no bad thing for a new artist.

### (iv) The Mate

The 'mate' is one step down from the enthusiastic amateur. Usually a person who knows one or more members of a band (or maybe one of the band's relatives), the mate will be glad to help out with carrying gear, putting up posters and organising gigs, but ultimately knows nothing about management and very little about the music business. Some mates do stay with a band as its career progresses, perhaps as roadie or by running the fan club. On no account sign a contract with a mate, or in fact put anything in writing at all!

# Management Agreements

If a manager is going to devote time, effort and occasionally even money to further the career of his artist, he is naturally going to want an agreement with that artist which will reward him for his efforts. Management contracts have enormous scope for unfairness, illegality and sharp practice. Artists have been known to almost sign their lives away in their desperation to advance their careers. Some of the shadiest characters in the history of the music business have been managers.

The reality of negotiating management agreements largely comes down to bargaining power. To be blunt, if you have attracted the attention of a major management company with a roster of successful artists and offices in other territories, they are less likely to compromise on the terms they want than a less successful manager who works from his mum's spare room.

There are two important rules

1.  You must never, ever sign a management agreement (or any other agreement for that matter) without taking the advice of a qualified music-business solicitor.

    To expand on this point, it is of no use whatsoever if somebody in your family knows someone who is a solicitor, or may be a solicitor themselves. Unless they are expert in music industry agreements and customs, they are unlikely to know what they are doing.

2.  You must never have the same solicitor as your manager.

Any manager worth his salt will want to manage you for as long as possible, and for the highest possible commission. He will want to be able to commission your earnings not only from music but from films, literary works and 'any other activities in the entertainment industry', or suchlike. Don't be put off by this; the manager is only trying to protect his earning potential at a time when the artist probably has little or no commissionable income.

# The Detail

Your lawyer will ensure that a reasonable agreement is negotiated, with the following main provisions:

## (i) The Term

The 'Term' means the length of time during which the manager will be acting as your manager. Somewhere between three and five years is acceptable, perhaps with a provision that the agreement may be terminated at the artist's discretion – say, after 12 months – if the manager has not secured interest from record companies (or publishers) or an actual deal.

## (ii) Commission Rate

Normally, the manager will expect between 15% and 20% of an artist's gross earnings (ie earnings before tax or any other deduction). As we will see later, the exception is gigging, where, due to the high costs involved, the commission should be based on a net-income formula, but with some kind of minimum percentage of the gross so that the manager can at least project what they are going to earn for the (often enormous) amounts of work that may be required of them during a tour. Many tours run at a loss, despite reasonable fees being paid by promoters, and it would be unfair for a manager to commission a loss-making venture at full rate.

The manager will want to commission all of your income from all possible sources on the basis that his efforts will hopefully put you in a position to be offered work not just connected with music. It is important to note that managers will wish to earn commission on recordings and songs for a period after they have stopped managing you. Examples of commissionable income would include income derived from live gigs, recording and publishing advances, royalty payments, PRS payments, personal appearances, DJing, TV and radio appearances, merchandising, sponsorship and record production.

In the case of recordings made (and songs written) during the Term, all managers will wish to continue receiving their commission on income that arises from those recordings and songs after the Term has ended, for a period of years. This is not unreasonable – after all, the artist, record company, publisher, producer and so on are continuing to earn – and the only issue will be for how long the manager can continue to receive their piece. All lawyers will suggest compromises whereby the commission rate reduces over a period of time and eventually the right to receive commission ends.

Whether your manager accepts this is really down to their bargaining power. If you write a huge-selling song, it is probably unfair that, five years down the line, some new manager who had nothing to do with your career when the song was a hit starts to receive commission on it. Similarly, it is unfair that your old manager, who will have been instrumental in your career at the time that you wrote the hit, should suddenly receive nothing. As with every negotiation, there will be a compromise.

The great battleground of management agreements is usually 'net or gross'. For those unsure of what this means, the following example should illustrate the potential pitfalls.

Let's say your manager agrees that you should do a gig for a flat fee of £1,000. His commission is 20% on gross, so he sends you a bill for £200. You have £800 left. Your agent who booked the gig gets his commission (see later) of 15% on gross as well, so you owe him £150. You have £650 left. The expenses for doing the show cost you a total of £750. You have thus spent £1,100 but have earned only £1,000 – you have lost £100 and have no income from which to make up this shortfall. If the manager commissions on net, however, and you still pay the agent his £150 on gross, you have only spent £900 (£750 gig expenses plus £150 agent's commission), which means that you have made a net profit of £100. The manager will then send you a bill for 20% of this net figure, ie £20. Big difference.

## (iii) Expenses

The manager will be expected to pay his office expenses (such as his office rent and electricity bill, for example) from his own pocket (ie his commission), but the artist will pay for everything else on top of the commission. A fixed sum – say, £250 for any one expense – should be built in to the deal over and above which the artist should specifically approve the expense, and often a maximum monthly limit. For example, you will have to pay the airfare if your manager flies to the US to conclude a deal for you. Difficulties can arise here where a manager is looking after more than one client, and it is almost impossible to gauge down to the last cent whether particular expenses have been incurred on business solely to do with you or connected with your manager's other clients.

To be blunt, if you – as opposed to your manager – control the band's money, then at least you're bargaining from a position of strength.

Many artists and their lawyers get overly worked up about expenses. At the end of the day, these should be reasonable, according to the financial position of the artist. The reality is that, if your manager worked for ICI rather than you and got a taxi to a meeting, he or she would put in an expense claim for the taxi bill.

## (iv) Financial Terms

Managers will normally wish to open and control a bank account in your name, receive income on your behalf and send you detailed accounts on a regular basis. Ensure that you are entirely happy with these arrangements, as they are the essence of the trust you will place in your manager. If you haven't done so already, delegate the task of keeping track of your finances to one band member.

The danger here is that unscrupulous managers have been known to steal their clients' money, 'borrow' it temporarily or deduct expenses that the artist has had no opportunity to verify or approve. Assuming that the artist is financially responsible and able to deal with the necessary administration, it may be safer to specify that funds don't get paid to the manager but are instead paid directly to the artist. The manager can then bill for his commission or expenses.

Bigger artists who are trading as a partnership, or through one or more limited service companies, usually retain a full-time accountant to receive funds on their behalf and handle all payments to third parties, such as managers. However, as

Sting discovered several years ago, even accountants acting for the artist are not immune to temptation.

## (v) The Manager's Obligations

This will be a general paragraph stating that the manager will use his best (or 'reasonable') endeavours to advance the artist's career, perhaps with specific objectives listed, such as getting the artist a record deal or gigs.

## (vi) The Artist's Obligations

These can be numerous, both general and highly specific. Examples might be that the artist should turn up promptly at recording sessions, or should not change his address or phone number without notifying the manager, or should not speak to the press without consulting the manager. The manager will also require the artist to warrant that he isn't contracted to anyone else for management, as, if he was, this would probably make his contract with the manager invalid.

## (vii) Other Provisions

You may wish to restrict the manager to managing only you, although it is unlikely that he will accept this limit on his potential earnings. Conversely, you need to ensure that you're getting enough of the manager's attention, particularly if he already manages a successful artist. The manager may wish to appoint a partner to co-manage you, perhaps for another territory, such as the USA. This, too, is not uncommon, although you must ensure that you have absolute approval over the choice of this person. The agreement will also include provisions dealing with what would happen if either party breached the contract.

## (viii) Power Of Attorney

'Power of attorney' means that one person has the authority to bind another person to do, or not do, something. If given to a manager, it would mean that he had authority to sign agreements on your behalf, perhaps without you being aware of the obligations contained in those agreements. An example might be an agreement with a promoter for you to go on tour.

It is never a good idea to give your manager a blanket power of attorney. Make sure you sign every contract or agreement yourself after you've read it carefully, and get into the habit of keeping a copy of it. This may be difficult if your manager is handing you huge sheaves of paperwork to sign the morning after a heavy gig, but don't be rushed into signing things without reading them and asking questions. This is one good reason to have regular, sensible formal meeting between manager and artist where business matters can be discussed, contracts signed and so on.

The only exception might be that you could allow your manager to sign agreements on your behalf for one-off live appearances in the UK.

# Verbal Contracts

It's worth noting here that management agreements don't necessarily have to be written down. 'Management contracts' don't necessarily have to be some kind of formal agreement which everyone signs. In the age of email, it is all too easy for an artist effectively to agree to be managed by somebody, or at least to give somebody grounds to say that they are managing the artist.

Be very careful about what you write in emails. If a manager were to email you and mention in passing, 'I charge 25% of gross and take each artist's publishing,' and you were to reply, 'I've spoken to the band and that sounds OK to us,' for example, then, if you proceed to work together with that manager for a couple of months before getting around to negotiating a formal deal, your email reply will have made your lawyer's job even more difficult.

Beware that verbal contracts can be upheld, and if there is a so-called 'course of dealing' between the band and someone helping them out that implies that the helper is acting as the manager (for example, if you paid a mate 20% of a gig fee for helping out), then you may run into problems if a more serious manager becomes interested in you.

It's best to be absolutely straight with mates who are helping you out, however grateful you are for their help, if their activities border on management. If you don't want them to be your manager, tell them, and put it in writing to them that any work they do on behalf of the band is not by way of management. And make sure that they aren't emailing the world at large, referring to themselves as your 'manager'. Apart from any legal difficulties that this may cause, people in the industry – some of whom may be managers whose interest you may be trying to attract – will be confused over whether you have actually got a manager or not.

On a general level, be aware that, if people help you out and are seemingly glad to do so, they may have hidden agendas that could cause you contractual and financial difficulty later on. I am not advocating universal cynicism, but it is always wise to look for the hidden catch or the angle.

# Relationship Between An Artist And Manager

It is relevant to note here (as I have mentioned in the chapter on record companies) that artists do not 'work' for managers in the capacity of an employee. Instead, artists retain the services of a manager as a supplier of services, under the terms of the management agreement.

# Self-Management

It is fair to say that most artists who have had fallings-out with their managers have considered self-management, but in reality this rarely proves successful, either financially or creatively.

If one argues that the artist is a creative individual who needs to be allowed the freedom to develop artistically, then someone needs to handle the (often boring) nitty-gritty and administration involved in that artist's career, as well as acting as the link between the artist and the record label, publisher, agents and promoters.

The level to which an artist lets his manager involve himself in the creative aspects of his career is at his discretion, after all. The artist may flourish under the guidance of a 'Svengali' manager who controls all aspects of his career, from what time he brushes his teeth to which songs get recorded. Other artists simply require someone to take care of business, sort out problems and occasionally fight their corner for them.

Often, artists who appear to be self-managed actually have a legion of highly expensive lawyers, accountants and business managers behind them who may end up costing far more overall than a 20% commission and may lack the commercial instincts to take decisions without involving the artists in every last detail. Such people are also unlikely to have the passion for the success of their artists that characterises the best managers.

On another level, in certain areas record companies prefer to deal solely with a manager, rather than directly with the artist, especially if the going is getting tough. On many occasions, the manager's skill will lie in translating the record company's position into more palatable 'artist-speak' to prevent a small problem from developing into a serious dispute.

Any manager who has watched This Is *Spinal Tap* (and anyone who wants to get into the music business should be forced to watch it) will empathise with the hapless Ian Faith in his attempts to manage the band. Every single one of those incidents, and worse, has happened!

# Being A Manager

If your ambition is to be an artist manager, be prepared for a life of hard work with little thanks, and also consider seeking psychological help. Managers are not the most popular people in the industry, for which they perhaps have only themselves to blame after decades during which the only press that managers got was bad press, often for good reason.

You'll probably only ever earn less than your artists, never more, and will have to get used to seeing the success you've played a major part in generating taken for granted both by your clients and others. Success has many fathers, and failure usually has only one: the manager. You will be present at the euphoric stage when the band feel that they, and only they, have got themselves a deal, and you will be there at the bitter end when you can only sit back and watch everything fall apart.

If that sounds cynical, it is simply a by-product of the central uneasiness of the relationship between any artist and their manager. The manager works for the artist, yet on the other hand has to exercise a strong element of control over his supposed 'boss' in order to make anything happen. Although you would expect me to say this, I can only advise total honesty in your dealings with artists, both on a business level, in terms of money, and on a day-to-day level, in terms of the plan and how things are going. There are always two sides to every story, and for every manager in a pub tonight leaping up and down, shouting that the band's latest demo is bound to get them a deal, there is an A&R person putting another demo back in its Jiffy bag with a rejection letter.

Be a realist, and try not to develop the habit of promising things that may not happen. Be honest about your feelings. If the band are constantly asking what's happening about a particular subject, and there's no news, tell them there's no news. If you haven't had time to deal with something, tell them. If someone thinks that the demo or the gig was the worst thing they'd ever heard or seen, tell them. At least the band will know that you tell it to them straight and will hopefully respect you for that, not least because you will stick by them through the good times and the bad.

It's also important for inexperienced managers not to give the impression that they're seasoned experts in all aspects of the business. If, for example, you know very little about the gigging side of the industry, it's far better to be completely upfront about it than risk embarrassment and ridicule at a gig in front of your clients by not knowing the basics. One manager I recently encountered (to be fair, he wasn't a native English speaker) had no idea what a front-of-house guy did. More worryingly, he wasn't quite sure what a 'grand' was.

## Starting Out

Apart from those who have completed some kind of higher-education course, most people drift into artist management from the traditional backgrounds of being a former artist, or perhaps a college booker or a journalist. Through talking to most managers, you'll tend to find that there was one very special act for them which was the deciding factor in them taking the plunge and becoming a full-time manager. In reality, with only one or two new acts without a deal, new managers need some other source of income, which will hopefully be derived from another part of the industry. Many new managers find it surprisingly easy to pick up the management of an established act that has perhaps fallen on hard times. This is by no means a bad thing, even if the manager might accept that the act in question is unlikely to relive its former glories. Many established acts that have parted company with their managers may welcome the injection of enthusiasm that a new manager may bring, and for the manager the chance to work with an act with some commercial value (particularly on the live circuit) is a fast track to gaining a lot of industry contacts.

The International Music Managers Forum is an invaluable organisation for managers and the only serious vehicle for them to act in unison, share information and deal with many of the constantly changing issues with which the industry is faced, all of which ultimately affect the artists', and therefore their managers', livelihood. The IMMF offers numerous training courses, seminars and events designed to help new managers understand the industry, and maintains an invaluable guidebook, The Music Management Bible (also published by Sanctuary), which no new manager should be without. Despite the fact that many managers can't stand the sight of each other and exist in a dog-eat-dog world, there does exist a kind of grudging respect for anyone who can survive as a manager. The IMMF certainly provides new managers with something to feel part of, and joining it is certainly recommended.

Many professional managers and management companies do have vacancies for anyone who wants to help out in their offices – usually for a pittance or, indeed, nothing – particularly if the person in question has boundless enthusiasm, gets the beers in and starts taking some of the pressure off the manager.

## The Manager–Artist Relationship

On a day-to-day level, most artists will, at some stage, drive the most patient and level-headed managers to the brink of distraction. There are numerous reasons for this, perhaps the overriding one being that creative people are not usually noted for their reasonableness and organisational skills. It is also the case that artists who are thrust into the industry can develop a completely unrealistic view of what may or may not be likely to happen in their careers, and often don't really understand the full horror of the machine they have signed up to be part of. Unfortunately, one of the worst parts of a manager's job is translating the sometimes baffling moves of the artist's label or publisher into some kind of acceptable form.

To be fair to artists, it's not unreasonable to ask for a fairly constant feed of information from the manager about what's going on, particularly at the stage when the artist is unsigned and there is some interest from labels or publishers. Things move quickly, however, and it's if the manager is having to make five calls to every member of the band to give them the latest bulletin, this is counter-productive. Most professional managers learn through experience that concise communication is the key, whether by emailing everyone or, more importantly, holding regular meetings at which everyone can be brought up to speed quickly.

In a band situation, a new manager has to be extremely quick on the uptake in understanding the band dynamic – who the prime movers are, what jealousies and rivalries exist, who the peacemakers are. It can cause problems if the manager assumes that the lead singer is the leader of the band and defers to them in preference of the other members of the band. Similarly, it can be a problem to assume that the drummer will simply go along with what everyone else thinks, or that, if the manager tells one member of the band something, they will automatically pass it on the other members. The best managers are adept at understanding how to communicate with their artists and how to use information effectively.

It is vital to understand the dreams, aspirations and insecurities of artists and to discuss them, because only by doing so can the manager foresee potential problems and also make sure that nobody is labouring under massively unrealistic expectations without the opportunity for the manager to fine-tune them.

Expect a few rows along the way about expenses, creative issues and attitude, but try to bring such problems to a definite conclusion and then move on, rather than allow certain issues to rankle. Have regular meetings with your clients and make sure that they understand how things have moved on since the last meeting or, if they haven't, why they haven't.

Decide if you want to put your own money into the project and, if so, how you're going to get it back. If you're going to expect your expenses – for example, taxis to gigs, drinks for A&R men and promoters – to be paid back by the band at some point, keep meticulous records and receipts, and send the band regular statements of how much you expect back. If you invest by contributing to the costs of recording sessions, photos or gigs, make it clear that you expect to be repaid before any of the band. After all, you're not in the band; you work for them.

Before a single fiver leaves your pocket, you need to be completely straight with the artist on the basis upon which you're working. For example, if you decide to put up £1,000 for some studio time, clearly there is a risk that the band may never get a deal and therefore may never have the money to pay you back. However, if you then part company with the artist and another manager secures them a deal using the tracks you paid for (and, incidentally, in which you legally own the copyright), you should be reimbursed.

Equally, you may take the view that you're prepared to lose a certain amount of money in order to see if there is any interest in a particular artist, and you'll accept that this investment may never be repaid by the band if nothing materialises, simply because they won't have the funds to do so.

It's also very difficult for new managers not to fall into the trap of doing absolutely everything for their clients – being at every gig, helping with the load-in, changing guitar strings – but this has its pitfalls. Inevitably, there will be some gigs you can't make it to, and some things you won't be able to take care of. Some artists will take this as a sign that you're becoming less committed when nothing could be further from the truth. It's much better to give every member of the band responsibility for specific areas and keep them fully involved in order to generate the feeling that they 'own' their own career. Otherwise, you'll be making a rod for your own back if things take off and you're still expected to be involved in every minute detail.

One legendary manager, talking about artists, once said to me – rather ominously – 'These people are not your friends.' Actually, it is a fair point. It is very difficult to remain emotionally and socially detached from your artists, who after all are relying on you as their manager to steer them through the choppy waters of the industry. On the whole, however, it is best to maintain some kind of distance, and if you are committed to working with a particular artist, get a contract signed and stick to your guns on the terms you want, within reason. On a day-to-day level, make it clear from the start if certain things are a problem for you – for example, you may want to lay the law down that, unless it's extremely important, you don't want to receive phone calls at weekends.

Maybe use the analogy of a ship. The manager is the captain. Many artists reading this may assume that therefore they are the passengers. Actually, they are the ship.

New managers taking on new artists can only start with a plan and then try to stick with it, and remain aware at every stage that it is extremely unwise to insist that anything at all is definitely going to happen, but that lots of things might!

# Tour Managers

You might be aware of the expression 'tour manager' ('TM') but be uncertain as to how they fit into the role of a traditional manager. Tour managers are hired by managers, or sometimes directly by the artists, to perform many of the manager's functions on a day-to-day level when on the road. These will include getting the band from A to B, collecting gig fees, liaising with the record company about instore appearances and TV and radio promotion, booking hotels and flights, and tour budgeting, as well as general troubleshooting.

Some TMs also take on the role of 'production manager' for a tour, which effectively means that they are responsible for everything that happens onstage – the PA, lights, staging – and the logistics of getting it where it's meant to be. TMs will certainly be involved at an early stage of the budgeting of a tour, and will be responsible for maintaining the budget as the tour progresses, no doubt dealing with a maelstrom of cancelled shows, lost passports, unexpected flights home and constant moaning.

It's generally not the best use of a manager's resources to spend a huge amount of time on the road. At the early stages of a band's career, the manager will be at most gigs, often because there's no budget for a TM (or often a crew, either). Once things move ahead and a deal has been signed, the manager will be there at key shows and rehearsals but will leave the nitty-gritty to the TM. Apart from anything else, if you're a manager sat in your office in London, it's usually impossible for that night's terrible show in Dundee to be your fault – although some artists will find a way to argue that it was...

Many new artists find that the ideal person is a combined TM and sound engineer, not least because, on low-level tours, both jobs can be handled without too much trouble. Many of the world's top tour managers started out as sound engineers.

Another oft-overlooked function of the TM is to act as a kind of surrogate parent for the band, many of whom will not have spent long periods away from home or have visited foreign countries. To an inexperienced manager, finding a well-established TM who won't try to usurp the manager's position with the band is a source of incredible relief. The TM will certainly give the manager the inside track on how the band are feeling at any particular moment and will hopefully be able to head off any problems that are developing before they become serious.

Tour managers tend to be paid a straight wage rather than taking a commission, and they are often paid retainers by bigger artists when not on the road, so that they are on call if needed. Tour management tends to attract highly capable and organised individuals who are used to getting by on little sleep and spending most of an average year in hotel rooms, on planes or in production offices with only their laptop for company and wondering where that 500 Euros from the float went.

Often, a highly trusted tour manager will become an artist's full-time manager after spending so long working with him or her that a strong bond develops. The larger management companies often have in-house tour managers who work with all of the company's clients at some stage.

# Finding A Manager

Without wishing to be glib, it's often the managers that find the bands, rather than vice versa. The same suggestions apply as for approaching record companies, in that the artist needs to draw himself to the attention of the manager, perhaps with the added ingredient that the artist should pitch himself to management that seems to have a track record in a particular field of music.

Many management companies have their own scouts, and all have a huge range of contacts in the industry at every level so that, if there is a buzz about a particular artists, they will pick up on it very quickly.

Most professional managers tend to be based in London, but that's no suggestion that a manager based in another region is necessarily less effective than one in London.

The blunt truth is that any professional manager or management company, however great they think a new artist is, will take that artist on only if they think that there's a worthwhile chance of getting them a deal of some sort and earning some commission.

Artists who are already the subject of attention from labels and publishers often find that the label or publisher will steer them towards a particular manager, which is not necessarily a bad thing. It tends to mean that the company respects that particular manager's style and knows instinctively that he or she will be right for a certain project, usually because they have worked together in the past, thus saving time on developing a working relationship.

Often, word of mouth is the best way to start, plugging your contacts at venues and other bands for information about the better managers that they have come across on their travels. A list of management companies is provided as Appendix 3, and the MMF publishes a list of its members.

# CHAPTER 5

# THE DEMO, IMAGE AND APPROACHING RECORD COMPANIES

For the purposes of this section of the book, it is assumed that the band have little or no experience of studio recording and wish to produce a demo of sufficient quality with which to approach record companies, publishers and managers.

Hopefully, the preceding chapters have helped to build up an understanding of the music industry and how it all fits together. This chapter aims to move up to the sharp end of attracting the attention of the industry and getting a deal. In reality – and one has to be blunt about this – very few artists ever get a deal of any type simply as a result of popping their demo in a Jiffy bag and then their phone ringing off the hook with companies desperate to sign them. Most artists who get deals do so as a result of a 'buzz' building around them, coupled with a very strong demo in circulation, some key gigs and, most importantly, a manager orchestrating the whole thing.

Most of the areas covered by this chapter apply equally to approaching publishing companies.

# The Demo

Without wishing to state the obvious, if you have an exciting demo of three or four great songs, well recorded and well played, you're already leagues ahead of most artists out there. It's a simple truth that the vast majority of demos doing the rounds of the industry range from being merely OK through to depressingly awful. Anybody in the industry will tell you that they know almost immediately that they hear something good. Apart from some kind of chance recommendation going around the industry from somebody who has maybe seen you live, or perhaps somebody being intrigued by the band's name on a poster or in Time Out magazine, it really all starts with the demo.

## Preparing To Record Your Demo

The first stage is to analyse critically all of the songs you've written. Assuming that you're already gigging, you'll have an idea of which songs in the set go down best. However, using this as the only benchmark will require you to convert whatever appeals about the song in a live setting into a worthy recording of it.

You're aiming to record your three or four best songs. Resist the temptation to concentrate on your earlier songs just because they are more familiar to you than ones you wrote recently. Even more importantly, resist the temptation just to record and send out a demo for the sake of doing it. It has to be special. People remember artists' names, and if you bombard the industry with material that isn't your absolute best then you'll have made the worst possible start.

Once you've identified your best songs, examine the arrangement, instrumentation and lyrics of each song. Be critical: Is there a strong chorus? Could the lyrics be made more interesting? One common mistake is to allow a song to become too long – for example, by leaving in unnecessarily self-indulgent solos.

Remember that your songs will have to grab people in their first 30 seconds. A&R people and managers are busy people and often wade through demos whilst in the middle of doing other things. Try to create an immediate impression. You may decide, for instance, to alter a song's arrangement so that it starts with the chorus. Also, avoid long, rambling, 'atmospheric' intro passages.

Finally, analyse the vocals and vocal melody. Try to vary the melody in each verse as the song progresses, and pay attention to the phrasing – don't try to cram in too many words in.

Once you've taken each song to bits and reassembled it, you should allow enough time for some serious rehearsals. If you've only ever been playing these songs at gigs, you may be surprised at how much 'improvisation' has crept in, with different members of the band misunderstanding their parts due to never having a good monitor sound (or monitors at all…).

If one of your songs features vocal harmonies, you may be able to save hours of wasted studio time by rehearsing all the harmonies at home so that everyone is absolutely clear about what they are singing.

By the end of the rehearsal, each member of the band should be able to play the songs in their sleep. Don't be tempted to add unnecessary instrumentation – the best songs are those that use space and atmosphere. As a final precaution, tape some rehearsals on a ghetto blaster and listen back to them the next day to be quite sure the band is tight.

# Choosing A Studio

In recent years, largely due to the proliferation of home computers, it has become less common for bands to take the traditional route of going into a local studio to record their initial demos. Many bands record at home, perhaps having laid down basic rhythm tracks onto disk in a local rehearsal room. Having said this, if the budget is available, using an engineer in a reasonably well-equipped studio will provide focus and will have the benefit of involving someone other than the artist, thus providing some objectivity. The other hidden benefit of using a traditional studio is that, to this day, many A&R people talk to respected studios quite regularly to ask if they have had any interesting clients through the door.

There is no rule that says that you can't record a great demo at home on basic analogue equipment or using a computer, especially if you use drum programming rather than try to mic up live drums. Remember, though, that most A&R people have reasonably high-quality hi-fis in their offices and that excessive hiss and distortion will be an immediate turn-off. If you're intending to use a traditional studio, it's probably true to say, therefore, that eight-track recording is the bare minimum. Sixteen-track is ideal, and 24-track may be over-complicating matters and be too expensive.

If you're a gigging band, you'll already be aware of what the best local studios are. Visit them all and get a feel for each place and its in-house engineer. You could play him your rough rehearsal tapes and see how quickly he cottons on to your description of your ideal sound. Don't be over-impressed if the studio has tons of outboard gear; none of it will turn a bad song into a good one. And be wary of jaded engineers who have demoed so many hopeless bands that they take little interest in your recording.

Studio rates are extremely competitive at present, and you should be able to negotiate a good 'lockout' deal at most places – ie you will be able to work for as long as you want each day, perhaps with a limit of, say, 15 hours. Steer clear of cut-price 'overnight' rates, particularly if you're working during the day, as your performance won't be up to scratch during these times.

Make quite sure that you know what you're paying for. Check the studio's price for CDRs and master tape. Ideally, if you can afford it, buy your multitrack tape or digital masters from the studio, as this way you keep control of your master and have the opportunity to remix it in the future. Be careful to check if the prices include VAT, and don't assume that you can use the studio's instruments free of charge. Be aware also that some studios will charge a fee if you use your own CDRs, DATs and other tape stock.

Be realistic about your budget and the amount of time you are allocating to get everything finished. It's better to have three fantastic tracks fully finished than two finished and two half-finished, and clock-watching during the session if the money is running out will not produce a good result. It's very important to discuss with the engineer what you're hoping to achieve in advance of the session, so that you don't try to overreach yourselves.

Work out how long your sessions are going to be and what you're going to do about meals – don't just live on Mars bars from the studio's machine! Also, check basic common-sense factors: Will your drum kit fit into the live room? Does the rhythm section need to play together to get it right, and, if so, is there enough space?

Once you've chosen your studio, worked out how much the demo will cost and planned the recording timetable, you need to check your instruments. Make sure that guitar leads work and are of good quality, and that guitars are earthed properly and do not buzz or hum. Check that your guitars are set up properly and play cleanly. You should have spare strings of different gauges, spare drum heads in case disaster strikes – in fact, spare everything. One common problem is that the drum kit doesn't record particularly well, and here, if the studio kit is similar and the drummer has no problem in playing it, it may save more money in time than it costs in hire fees to use it. Another candidate for not recording well are the acoustic guitars, so bring any spares you have and any you can borrow in order to give you some choices if yours isn't sounding that great.

There's nothing worse than spending money on a demo and the end product being a disappointment. By preparing properly, you will avoid wasting unnecessary time and money.

# Recording And Mixing

Arrive at the studio early to begin setting up. Let the engineer do his job and mic up drums and amps the way he wants them, unless you have a strong preference in this area.

Don't spend too long on getting sounds – you're not going to get a record deal just because you've got a great snare sound – and try to put down as good a guide vocal as possible early on in the recording; you may be able to keep most of it, with a few patch ups. Don't be afraid of using samples – the engineer may have exactly what you want on disk, which will save loads of time; there's no point being a luvvy just because it isn't 'your' sound. Try to go for as 'live' a sound as possible to emphasise the song itself rather than the production. And don't spend too long on the mix – keep it simple, but make sure there's a nice vocal sound above everything. A&R people will be listening out for songs, but great voices as well. I would recommend spending an hour or so on getting a reasonable monitor mix of each track, then going away for at least a few days before returning to do the proper mix.

It tends to be the case that the best demos are produced when as much time is left for mixing as for recording, as the most frequent problems concern instrumental balance in the mix. Undoubtedly, every member of the band will want to be heard above everyone else, especially if everyone has paid towards the recording, and this is a common area of dispute. If one element isn't loud enough, turn everything else down rather than turn one instrument up. If at all possible, one band member should bring in a pair of speakers that they are familiar with, and the band should all listen to a CD they all know over them to get an idea of how the room and monitors colour the sound.

Don't be too precious about who is doing the harmonies – use whoever sounds best. It doesn't matter if you don't sing it like that live; you're trying to make the best-sounding demo possible.

It's a good idea to do three mixes of each song: a well-balanced mix, the same mix but with the vocal up, and a mix with no vocal (often called a 'TV track') is always useful. Avoid mixing too loud, as this is misleading, and finally pile on the compression before the final mix goes down to CDR/DAT, as this will add punch.

Remember that engineers are not producers, and while a good engineer may take a minor creative role in the proceedings – perhaps by suggesting which take of a song is best – most will take a back seat and not make their day more difficult than it already is.

Once the mix is finished, have the final payment ready so you can take your master material away. Just before putting the mixes down to DAT/CDR, try playing the final mix on a car stereo or ghetto blaster, or even a mono tape player, to ensure that it sounds good. Don't play it at ridiculously high volumes – everything sounds better like that!

Take a master CDR of the final mixes and, if your software is compatible with the studio's, take a copy of the individual parts so you'll be able to have a go at doing any necessary remixes at home.

# The Acid Test

Each member of the band should play the demo to as many friends and relatives as possible immediately it is finished. You will quickly get a feel for what the 'favourite' track is. This is important, as you must put the best song first on the demos you'll be sending out. If necessary, resequence your CDR before running off the copies you'll be sending out.

# Packaging The Demo

Some of this may seem obvious advice, but sometimes it's easy to overlook the obvious.

Get a reasonable number – say, 100 – CDRs duplicated from the master CDR. Use a professional duplication facility, if one exists locally. If you have to post your master somewhere, take a copy and use registered post.

If you can afford it, get the inlay cards and label printed by the duplication facility and include the name of the band, the song titles and, most importantly, a contact name and phone number. Writing the contact info on the inlay card alone is useless as CDRs often get separated from their cases.

Try to make the inlay card interesting. Photoshop – a computer graphics application – can do wonders for presentation. Again, include the contact details, the names of the band members and instruments played, and who wrote the songs. Avoid including detail about when the demo was recorded; if you're still sending it out in a year's time, it will seem dated and raise the presumption that you've done nothing new since.

Ensure that the contact number is constantly manned, if you haven't got an answering machine or a mobile with voicemail. If an A&R person should call, it's not going to leave a particularly good impression if he gets through to the drummer's grandma!

Although it may be a pain, listen to each CDR before you send it off. If one is faulty, that just may be the one that could have got you some interest, so it's worth the effort. If you want your demos to be returned if the recipients aren't interested, include the band's address on the label and inlay card.

SANCTUARY

1. **Here She Comes** (Smith/Jones)
2. **All Over The World** (Smith/Jones)
3. **Song 3** (Smith/Jones)

**Contact:** Mike Anager 01234 567890
(mobile) 0207 345 6789 (office)

© 2005 The copyright in these sound recordings
is owned by Sanctuary – All rights reserved.
All songs written by Smith/Jones. All songs copyright control.

## HOW A CD
## LABEL SHOULD LOOK

It goes without saying that CDR is now the standard format on which people in the industry would expect to receive a demo. Clearly, it is also possible to send songs to people on MP3, but in practice any A&R person whose email address has been clogged up with hundreds of MP3s from unknown artists is going to take a fairly dim view of an unsolicited music file.

# Image

Image is difficult to define. Sometimes the most image-conscious artists are those who appear to have no image at all, yet move seamlessly with the times in the way they present themselves, making subtle changes as the years pass.

Others rely on complete overhauls of look and style with almost every new album – Madonna and David Bowie, for example – until their image becomes almost more important than their music. Others still – Bryan Adams and Bruce Springsteen, for example – choose to project a consistent and unchanging image as ordinary Everymen whose look reflects that of their idealised audience.

Anyone reading the music media for more than ten years will realise that all styling is essentially cyclical and rarely truly original. Skinny ties are back for at least the third time I see...

Some would argue that image is something that you either have or you haven't, yet on the other hand the industry is full of highly paid stylists whose function it is to mould the image of artists into whatever saleable form is required. It is difficult to offer positive advice about image, as it is a purely subjective area. At present, the look adopted by most serious artists is anti-style, whilst pure pop artists, as always, simply reflect whatever current fashion and grooming is decreed to be right for their audience. It's all too obvious when new artists are simply trying to ape the image of their favourite bands, however, and such attempts are usually doomed to heroic failure. There are few things more sad than seeing photos of new bands failing to recreate the images of their heroes, images that have taken thousands of pounds' worth of styling and photography to present, so try to avoid this at all costs. To the jaundiced eye of an experienced A&R man or manager, it's not just that you look sad; it's also the fact that you clearly haven't realised it that's the problem!

On a serious note, errors of judgement in image and styling will simply detract from your music, which is what you're trying to draw attention to in the first place.

# Photographs

All artists need to hold a photo session reasonably soon after they start working, and some basic mistakes here are fairly easy to avoid. With the huge advances in digital photographic technology in recent years, it should be possible for even the most basically competent photographer to get some useable band shots.

If possible, you should use a professional photographer who has an interesting and creative portfolio, or investigate any local photography courses to see if there is a student there who is inclined towards working with bands. All local papers have staff photographers, some of whom may have taken interesting band shots before.

Whatever you do, don't have your picture taken in front of your mum's living-room curtains on some cheap domestic camera – this is completely pointless if you're serious about your music. Also, live shots from gigs are rarely any use, due to the low lighting involved and the impossibility of posing properly for shots.

Good band photos don't have too much background and concentrate on the band's faces. Avoid shots of the band standing meaningfully in the middle distance, which will make everyone's features tiny when reproduced in 5" x 7" format. Look at professional shots of bands in the music press, and if you see something you like then ask the photographer to try something similar. Black-and-white tends to look classier than colour, although some local papers now refuse to print anything other than colour pictures.

Once the best shot is agreed upon, you'll need to get some photos duplicated and also have the ability for any interested media contacts to download the best shots from your website or have them emailed to them. For hard copies, the more you duplicate, the cheaper per print it gets. It's possible to kill two birds with one stone and get postcard-quality reproductions, which can also carry information on the reverse and act as gig flyers. Ensure that the postcards contain as much information as possible. The front of the card should simply have the picture and name/logo and website address. On the back, have the logo again, plus the band's postal and website addresses, but leave a space between them on the left-hand side for handwriting, and on the right for people's addresses. Duplication normally takes about two weeks.

Incidentally, it seems to be the rule that one member of the band will decide to leave immediately after the first photo session, so make sure that every member of the band has some individual shots taken as well. You can always make a composite version for a demo inlay or the website, in this case.

# Approaching Record Companies

Majors and the larger independents receive literally hundreds of demos every week from people all over the UK and often abroad. As previously mentioned, bands almost never get a deal solely on the strength of their demo; there has to be a combination of factors that go together to create a 'buzz'. These include:

- Recommendations from respected managers, DJs, promoters, producers, studios, venues, agents, lawyers and journalists.

- Reviews in the national press, and on websites respected by the industry.

- TV and radio appearances.

- Gigging in London.

Taking advantage of these factors is covered in Chapter 6, 'Self-Promotion And Gigs'. We'll concentrate here solely on sending in your demo.

Your demo package needs to contain the following:

1. Demo, with inlay card.

2. Photo of band.

3. Covering letter.

   Keep the covering letter brief, as A&R people are busy people. Address it to the A&R person by name, and write it on specially headed band paper. Here's some suggested wording:

'Dear...

Please find enclosed the latest demo from [name of band in capitals]. As you'll see from the attached biog, we're starting to get quite a live following locally and will be gigging in London shortly. We hope you'll like the songs enough to come and see us live, and we'll put you on our guest list. Best wishes...'

Don't ramble on unnecessarily and try to get the letter typed as opposed to handwritten.

4. Biography.

One side of an A4 sheet is enough. Include the names of the band members, who plays what, how long the band have been going, where you've been gigging, who you've supported, how big the crowds were and where the demo was recorded, and list your forthcoming gigs, including the addresses of the venues, their phone number and what time you'll be on. Don't bother with tedious explanations of the lyrics, what effects pedals you used and what other local bands you've all been in (unless they achieved anything noteworthy).

Once you've sorted out the above four items, send them off in a padded envelope addressed to the A&R person by name. Make up a chart of who you've sent demos to, and on what date, and keep a track of the responses you get and who is being particularly slow in getting back to you.

# Who Are The A&R People?

A&R staff change jobs fairly regularly, so I've avoided listing specific names in Appendix 1, which lists most of the more significant record companies in the UK. Once your package is ready, it's far better to send it to an individually named A&R person than just address it to 'The A&R Department'.

It is possible to phone up A&R departments without making a complete pest of yourself. All you need to establish in about 30 seconds of conversation with an (undoubtedly harassed) A&R secretary is who is the best person to whom you should send your demo.

If you think that you sound similar to (or reviewers have noted similarities with) a particular band signed to a label, phone and ask who the band's A&R person is and send the demo to him. If you're creating music in a very specific musical genre – say, dance, guitar pop or heavy rock – describe your sound to whoever answers the phone and they will probably suggest a name to address the package to. Whether or not the named person is just the person who listens to all unsolicited demos, or whether your demo will get slung onto their pile anyway, is impossible to say, but at least make sure you ask how his or her name is spelled!

# Points To Note

All demos get listened to. Eventually. By 'listened to' I mean that, unless the package looks particularly interesting or the A&R person is feeling particularly conscientious that day, the first song will be listened to for 20 seconds, maybe fast-forwarded for a minute in an effort to find the chorus, and then will be lobbed back in the package for the secretary to send back with a rejection letter.

Many record companies insist that the A&R secretaries keep a log of demos received and what the response was.

You are unlikely to hear anything for a month.

There's no real point in ringing up A&R people to see what they think of the demo, or if they've got it. If they like it, they'll ring you.

A&R offices deal with a lot of nutters: housewives who send in tapes of their budgie whistling, pub singers sending in versions of 'It's Not Unusual', people singing along to Whitesnake or on their own in the bathroom – the list is endless. There are a lot of weird people out there. This goes some way to explaining the somewhat terse response phone calls receive.

Call A&R departments a week before your London gigs to see if anyone is coming, or better still fax/email them a note about the gig.

Don't be depressed if you get a standard rejection letter. Some of the biggest bands in the world today could wallpaper a room with the rejection letters they once received.

If an A&R person calls you and wants to hear some new material, send them some, not some old sub-standard stuff. Send it quickly and ring them to say it's on the way, and mark the outside of the package with the name of the band and the words 'requested material'.

Always put any A&R person who's shown an interest on the guest list for every gig you do, plus one.

On no account bombard A&R people with endless emails, or MP3s, unless they specifically ask you to send them some material.

# Meeting A&R People

If your demo has attracted a call from an A&R person, you can already afford yourself some level of congratulation, without getting your hopes up. Some will call simply to ask for more material, and perhaps to say that they might come along to the next gig.

If you're a regional artist, and an A&R person is venturing out of London to see you, you're clearly worthy of serious interest.

Some A&R people like to meet up with almost every band they're interested in, at least for an exploratory chat. In doing so, they are aware that the band will be setting great store by the meeting and will already be having visions of getting signed. This places a subconscious pressure on the A&R person before the band have even walked into a room, so how artists handle themselves at these meetings is important.

You should be prepared to take constructive criticism of the songs and the recordings. After all, you're meeting someone who gets paid for making such judgements, whether you agree with them or not. Be prepared to talk about your influences, and about how you see your career progressing – be positive without resorting to Gallagher-esque bluster.

The A&R person may already have seen you live and may have distinct views on the way you presented yourself on stage. The frontman or -woman is likely to feel quite defensive at this point, but try not to make excuses if the gig in question wasn't a great night.

Remember also that most A&R people will be eager to talk about what they're currently working on and recent successes they might have had. It's worth finding out as much in advance as you can about the person you're going to meet, as it will help the atmosphere of the meeting if you appear to be equally interested in what they're doing as they are in you. After all, this might be the person with whom you develop an incredibly close working relationship with over many years, and first impressions count.

If things are going well between the two of you, you could suggest that the A&R person's company put up a demo budget for you to enable you to record some further tracks. (All major A&R departments have demo budgets.) If they agree, the A&R person may put you into a London studio with a name engineer to see what you're capable of producing. Publishers are less likely to agree to fully fledged demo budgets, although many have their own small demo studios in which they may offer you some time.

At all costs, try to leave the meeting with a definite idea about what to do next, and how to move things along with the A&R person, rather than vague promises to send more material or keep in touch. It is therefore vital that, before arranging meetings, several confirmed gigs are booked in your diary for the weeks and months after the meeting, so that you can firm up the A&R person's attendance at these, there and then.

# Networking

The music industry depends on networking to an enormous extent. Assuming that you're based in London, if you are out and about seeing gigs, meeting other bands, playing shows and rehearsing, inevitably you will begin to meet people from the industry. These will either be promoters, record-company or music-publishing A&R people, journalists, or agents. More often than not, these meetings will just be a matter of happenstance, and will usually take place at a gig or in a pub.

If you take an interest in the goings-on in the music industry – for example, by reading Music Week – then you will already be familiar with some of the key players and the key companies who should be on your target list. By networking, you're simply trying to develop a list of contacts that will be of use to you.

Without spraying them around like confetti, it's always a good idea to carry a couple of CDRs of your latest songs around, or a recent single release, for the simple reason that any brief chat with someone will usually sign off with 'Send me some stuff, then,' or 'I'll send you some stuff,' and then five minutes later neither person is quite sure who the other person was, what their band was called, what company they work, for and so on. At least by giving them a CD there and then you'll have increased the chances of it getting heard.

Similarly, it's a good idea to carry around business cards of some description, and also ask people if they have a card you could have. It's pointless trying to scrabble around for a pen when someone is trying to bellow their email address at you during a gig.

Try to strike a balance between appearing too pushy and too reticent. If you get talking to an industry person, find some common ground – you might know some of the same people – and ask about them, rather than tell them about you. If you can strike up some kind of rapport with them, you can always say, 'Have a listen if you want,' and give them a CD. Keep it casual. At the end of the day, they will either like it or not. Nobody likes the pressure of some desperate band member or manager thrusting CDs at them 30 seconds after being introduced.

# Showcases

Doing a 'showcase' for industry people – either a specially arranged gig in a proper venue or a private performance in a rehearsal room – can be a nightmarish experience, but they are often necessary to firm up any interest from A&R (or for them realise that it was all bullshit in the first place, it has to be said).

Often, showcases are arranged – often at significant expense – more in the hope than the expectation that an A&R person who has expressed only a mild interest will show up. A&R people are notoriously flaky when it comes to arranging their diaries and have little regard for the fact that, if they cancel a meeting or fail to show up at a showcase, the band may have lost a packet in getting there. On the other hand, if there is significant interest in a band, a showcase can signify the start of a bidding war between different labels and publishers. Additionally, labels will sometimes fund a private showcase themselves in order to check that the band can really cut it.

Showcase gigs at proper venues have the advantage of (hopefully) having a built in audience, but they are prone to the usual gig hassles and technical hitches. Also, if only a small crowd shows up, through no fault of the band – it might just be a rainy night, or the football might be on TV – the atmosphere will be depressing, as the A&R person will secretly be hoping to be privy to a sold-out show by the next big thing. And if you're wondering, all new bands anxiously scan the guest list after their set has ended to see if so-and-so turned up, all try to work out why they haven't if they haven't, and all managers feel a kind of crestfallen defensiveness at this point.

All managers and bands blatantly fib about the time they are supposedly on stage. They will say 8:15 when it is, in fact, 8:30 in the hope that the industry people (even if slightly late) will arrive in time to catch the whole set. This can be totally counter-productive if things end up running late and you don't go on until 9, because your target people might have had to leave. All industry people get very disgruntled if they've turned up to see a band, and the band before them has only just gone onstage. Their ideal situation is to walk into the gig and get a drink at the precise moment the band go onstage. Personally, I would always prefer any industry person to see a new artist 'first on', simply because they will have soundchecked last so everything should sound good, the start time is usually fixed, and any lack of a crowd can be blamed on the headliners!

At least in a rehearsal room you will have the chance to get everything sounding good before anyone arrives. Invite a few mates along for a bit of atmosphere and encouragement, and run through the set a few times to get a feel for the monitor sound in the room. Do four or five songs – all the ones that the A&R person has said he likes – and then maybe throw in a strong new one to give him the impression he's being given a sneak preview.

If you're in the fortunate position of having a few A&R people interested, stagger their arrival times throughout the day, by all means, but don't worry if they occasionally bump into each other. They all know which bands each other is interested in.

It is sad but true that all A&R people fall prey to a strange sheep-like mentality as soon as they know that one of their rivals is pursuing a particular artist. It is as though they need to be convinced that they may lose the artist before they get really interested. Your manager will, of course, take full advantage of this by casually dropping rivals' names into his conversations with labels and publishers, and generally stirring up the rumour mill as much as possible, aided by your lawyer.

As soon as one label or publisher makes an offer, your manager and lawyer will waste no time in telling any rivals what the offer is in the hope of starting a bidding war for your signature. Obviously, this is an extremely fortunate position to be in, particularly nowadays, when there is little on offer in the way of huge advances. But a word of caution is necessary. Whatever the fine detail of £10,000 here or there by the time you get to the advances for the second album (which, incidentally, you may never get to anyway), you will probably have a gut instinct for which company and A&R person will be most creatively in tune with you and easiest to get on with very soon after meeting them for the first time. Be wary of your manager simply gravitating towards the deal with a bit more money on the table and instead look at the long-term picture.

# CHAPTER 6

# SELF-PROMOTION AND GIGS

## Self-promotion

The term 'self-promotion' encompasses anything a band can do to advance its career and profile, build a 'buzz' and thus bring the chance of a deal closer. Some of the suggestions contained in this chapter are reasonably expensive, while others require only time and effort. Many of the suggestions relate to making the most from gigging, and their benefits will increase with the number of gigs performed.

Like image, the 'buzz' is difficult to define, but you know it when you've got it! Put simply, it's when the industry as a whole begins talking about a particular artist, from journalists beginning to take an interest through to A&R people coming down to gigs, calling back and setting up meetings. Only rarely does a buzz develop on the basis of a demo alone, but rather as a result of the increasing visibility of a particular artist on the live circuit and in the media, and perhaps from some kind of independent release. It means that even lawyers have heard of the band! Once the buzz is going around the industry, the band are basically in the box, with an open goal in front of them. If the talent and the determination are there, they should score; if the moment passes, then maybe they were never going to score in the first place.

Your aim, as a new band, should be to build your local audience as rapidly as possible and at the same time increase your local press profile, before moving on to develop a national profile.

In doing so, it helps to have an ongoing understanding of developments in the industry on a week-by-week basis, and for this purpose I would strongly suggest subscribing to the industry magazine *Music Week* (www.musicweek.com). Whilst this book has hopefully given you some insight into how the industry works and how to use this information to your advantage, it is a great help to learn about the personalities within the industry, the new labels being set up and the ones closing down, as well as to see detailed information on market statistics, including the sales and airplay charts. It isn't cheap to subscribe to Music Week, but absolutely everyone in the industry reads it and it may give you a certain edge.

Let's start with the basics.

# Band Names And Logos

It's important for a new band to establish its identity quickly, and so a striking yet simple logo is vital. Most people now have access to adequate PC or Mac systems, which can be used to create something memorable. Failing this, a local print shop or design house may charge very little to work on a band logo, as it's slightly more interesting than designing the menu for the local kebab house.

Avoid complicated designs that might look great close up but would be completely indecipherable from across the street, and resist the temptation to copy the style of a well-known band. Have a good think about the band's name as well – because of compactness, 'U2' can be printed in huge letters on a poster. You can't say the same for 'And You Will Know Us By The Trail Of Dead...', despite it being a memorable name!

One key early question is whether or not the suggested name is available as a domain name for the band website. If it isn't, you should consider not using it rather than trying some adaptation of it as the website address, particularly if the precise domain name belongs to some totally irrelevant site.

Names that involve numbers are also confusing, as over the phone people won't know whether to use the numeric or lettered version. Bear in mind also that the name should be easy to pronounce in any language, and difficult to misspell – you'd be surprised how irritating this gets after a while! Choosing a band name can take a considerable amount of time, and I would advise living with it for a while before definitely settling on it. It may just 'look' wrong on a T-shirt. It may sound...just boring. Or really sad. There has been a craze over the last couple of years for bands to be named 'The...', but most people seem to think that this has been done to death now. Try not to use words which are linked with products, services or organisations, as you may be getting into legal difficulties, and try to resist using something particularly offensive because, although it might seem extremely provocative and anarchistic to you at the time, this will wear off rapidly if people simply refuse to play you on the radio or put your name on a poster.

It's a complicated and expensive procedure to register a band's name as a trademark or registered mark, although most bands of any stature whose merchandise is worth pirating have done so. However, you want to be sure that your band name is original and protected as far as it can be. Once you have thought of a name, search for it online and make sure nobody else is using it, then register it at www.bandreg.com. This will at least provide some evidence that you thought of it on a certain date.

Once you've done this, keep all of your early press mentions with dated newspaper cuttings, and download and file all online mentions of the band so that, in the event of a dispute with another band, you may be able to claim first ownership. If your career extends to the USA, then there is an even greater likelihood that almost any name will have been used before, which will require yours to be altered. For example, The Charlatans are known in the USA as 'Charlatans UK'.

Ultimately, once you've chosen a name, you'll want to stick with it, so it's best to go through the rigmarole at the outset than risk having to start all over again once you've built up a bit of momentum.

# Website

No serious artist or band can afford to be without a website, full stop. The Internet has become the first port of call for anyone even mildly curious about any artist, and (apart from a chance encounter at a gig or a mention in the press) the band website will tend to be the industry's (and the public's) first meaningful experience of the band.

For this reason, it is vital to create and maintain an effective, stimulating and regularly updated website, and to invest the time and money required to do this.

For any new band, the primary functions of the website can be summed up as Music, Mailing List, News. The band needs to communicate with its audience about forthcoming gigs and anything else of interest, and needs to do this not only by putting up news on the site but by building up a mailing list of its supporters, using music as the bedrock of the site.

Other functions of the site could be to act as a contact point for business enquiries, to provide a fan forum and to sell CDs and other merchandise.

The most effective band websites are stylish, quick to load and have a striking homepage. A brief checklist of the basic elements of a good site would be as follows:

## Home Page

This should be quick to load, feature striking images and maybe some music, and have either an 'Enter' button or a list of links.

## News Page

This can be broken down into areas such as news updates, a band diary and so on, with links to other relevant pages.

## Bio/Press

The band's biography and any relevant press quotes or interviews should be here, together with profiles of each band member, which should be made as interesting as possible.

## Gallery

This should contain studio shots, gig shots and maybe the facility for fans to send in their own pictures.

## Music Or Media

This should have excerpts of tracks and maybe one full track as a RealAudio or Windows Media file (ensuring that copyright information is listed), and perhaps a link to the CD-sales page. It could also feature some video footage, depending on the site's capabilities.

## Message Board

Either a forum or a guestbook, and the place to sign up for the mailing list.

## Shop

Hopefully, the place where the site makes some money, either by sales of CDs or merchandising, paid for via systems such as PayPal or via snail mail, using a downloadable order form.

# Local Press

Almost every local paper in the country – even the free sheets – has some form of music column that devotes some space to local bands. Make a list of all the local columns, including those in papers you might not buy, such as local college and university publications, fanzines, and local arts-centre leaflets – and call each one to ascertain who is the correct person to send information to.

Once you've prepared this list, put it into the computer in whatever format is suitable for printing sheets of sticky labels. This will save you hours of hassle in the future, as you won't have to write out envelopes by hand. Alternatively, you might be able to achieve the same result with an email mailshot.

Once you've got your list sorted out, it's time to compose your first press release.

The term 'press release' sounds like a rather grand thing for a new band to be issuing, but it's best to start as you mean to go along. Even if you've got no gigs booked, create a preliminary press release and send it, along with your demo and a photo, to each columnist. Make the press release as upbeat as possible but not too long. An example might be:

## PRESS RELEASE
### Date:
'[Name of band] are a new four-piece band from [name of town] comprising [name] (bass), [name] (drums), [name] (guitar/vocals) and [name] (lead vocals). The band was formed in 2005 from members of [name any relevant previous bands] and has just recorded a three-song demo [title of demo] containing original compositions [insert song titles].

'The band are currently lining up some local gigs, but in the meantime you can get more information from [band website address].'

At the bottom of the press release, but not for publication, put:

'For further press information and pictures contact [band phone number].'

Resist the temptation to bullshit wildly in your first press release. Probably the oldest chestnut is something along the lines of 'currently attracting major record company interest'. Seasoned local journalists have heard it all before, and their readers have read it 1,000 times. You're trying to get the journalist on your side.

Call each journalist a few days after you've sent the press releases out and check that they've received it, what they thought of the demo, and if they'll be printing a mention for the band. Most of them will not print anything at this early stage but will tell you that they'll do something when you've got some gigs to announce.

When you've sorted out some gigs, send out a new press release repeating the first part of the first press release just to remind the journalist who you are, then put in details of the gigs in the following format:

> Date: .......................................................................................
> Venue: ....................................................................................
> Phone Number: ....................................................................
> Door Time: ..........................................................................
> Price: ......................................................................................
> Other Bands: ......................................................................
> Your Stage Time: ................................................................
> Ticket Price/Concessions: ..................................................

Again, call each journalist a few days after you've sent this one out to check if the information is going in the paper, and this time ask if he or she wants to come to the gig. If this seems likely or possible, remember to put their name on the guest list, and check whether or not a 'plus one' is needed.

As your profile develops, the information you release about the band will need to become more eye-catching and interesting. With all due respect, 'Band Plays Gig' is hardly news. Look at the way online news and music press articles are written, and try to inject some zest into the information.

Local press can have a surprising impact, initially because many of your friends and relations will see it and take the band more seriously as a result. Occasionally, record companies will call up journalists on the larger local papers to see what new local bands are causing a stir, so your name needs to be at the top of the list.

Be sure to keep every little bit of local press you receive – you'll be surprised how it mounts up, and it will help you to get more gigs. Promoters will respect any band that understands the importance of getting itself in the papers. As your local profile increases, you should be asking some of the journalists who have taken a liking to the band if they'll do a feature on you to coincide with some major news, such as supporting a nationally known band or releasing your first indie single.

Local journalists are likely to be pleasantly impressed with a band that seems to be taking a professional approach to its presentation. Remember that many of these journalists are also on the mailing lists of the major record companies and so are used to seeing innovative and exciting packages. A supporter on the local paper can become one of your greatest allies and should certainly be someone you buy the occasional beer. And never forget that they might get a job at the NME next month!

## Local Television And Radio

Some regional ITV stations produce local arts programmes, as do the larger BBC regional centres. These shows almost invariably feature some music content, as well as national artists who may be touring in the region. Unless your band is becoming a local phenomenon and is attracting large audiences, it's unlikely that the producers of these programmes will give you preference over a Peruvian nose-flute player or a feature on basket weaving. However, nothing ventured, nothing gained, so call up your local TV station and ask if they are producing any local arts programmes in the coming year. If they are, you need to get through to the programme's production office and find out who the researcher or 'guest booker' for the show is, and then send them your demo and press cuttings.

The proliferation of satellite and cable channels in recent years has led to more opportunities for newer bands to gain some exposure. Although this might involve playing in front of one guy with a video camera at the local shopping mall, any exposure at this stage is worthwhile, especially if you can get a copy of the tape. One thing, though: try to mime on this kind of show, as playing live will usually fall foul of the somewhat limited technical set-ups available to smaller channels.

Radio is a more likely source of exposure. Local regional and college stations often have a weekly show (which you should already know about) devoted to local talent and which plays demos (as long as they are of reasonable quality), particularly if you can supply a CD. Failing this, if there is a particular local presenter who plays your kind of music, send him a demo and some info. You might not get played, but he might give one of your gigs a plug in his show.

## The National Music Press

As soon as you have even one gig arranged, you should be sending off a press release to the national weekly music press and, if it's far enough in advance, the monthly ones as well. The most you can hope for is a mention in the 'Gig Guide', but you may also get a mention in 'Tour News' if there are more than a few gigs. Always include a picture.

At the same time, make a note of the names of all the journalists on each national paper who seem into your brand of music, and send them an information pack with a demo addressed to them c/o the publication in question. However, don't send a demo – or indeed anything – if you're going to use the same tracks shortly afterwards on an indie release. It's better to wait. You might get a call from one of them asking if they can come down and review one of your gigs – and a review in the national press will be read by 99% of the A&R people in the country. Your name will enter their consciousness...

Press such as the NME and The Fly offer relatively cheap advertising rates, and, depending on your budget, this may be a worthwhile investment if you have a run of dates coming up or some kind of release.

# Posters

It almost goes without saying that posters are the cheapest and most effective way of promoting gigs. Despite it being illegal in many areas, flyposting is a common occurrence all over the UK. Recently, local councils have threatened flyposting companies with ASBOs (Anti-Social Behaviour Orders), and in some cases have actually prosecuted them in an effort to deter this activity, so think twice before doing it. However, posters can be given to promoters at club gigs, local record shops and youth clubs, so they are a useful tool, come what may.

An extremely striking black-and-white A3 poster can be produced on a photocopier, or you might want to get more creative by printing on fluorescent paper. Design one generic poster with a box space at the bottom for information such as gig dates or 'demo on sale here', etc.

Send every venue at which you're gigging two posters to put up well ahead of your gig. One word of warning, though: Cover up existing flyposters at your peril. Flyposting companies guard their sites jealously and tend to take a very dim view of anyone interfering with their business, which may involve large gentlemen wishing to have a quiet word with you! Far better – and safer – to make some discreet enquiries at venues and find out who the local flyposting operation is, and ask them what is the cheapest deal they'll do.

# Flyers

Flyers are A5 (ie half the size of A4) or smaller photocopied slips designed to be handed out at gigs or left on record shop counters. Make the design as striking as possible, with the band's logo printed as large as possible. Flyers can be easily photocopied by duplicating the design on both sides of one sheet of A4 and then guillotining the resulting copy. Always include the band website address on flyers, even if you're only advertising gigs and not your demo or merchandise.

If you can negotiate a reduced-price admission to the gig with the promoter for punters carrying flyers, then people have an incentive to pick them up and keep them.

# Mailing List

Starting a mailing list of your supporters is one of the most effective ways of building up a local fan base. This is absolutely vital for any new band, as people are apathetic enough about coming to gigs already, without giving them the excuse that they didn't even know about it. The old-fashioned method needs a postal address, a bit of time and effort, plus stamps!

At each gig, hand out your postcards (see the section on 'Photographs' in the previous chapter) to the audience. On the left-hand side you will have stickered (on a small white label) wording such as: 'Free Information Service. Please fill in your name and address on the right and hand this card in to the band at the end of the gig. We'll send it back to you with a free CD and let you know about any future gigs. Thanks for coming.'

You will note the words 'free CD'. This is optional, but if you have a good demo and can afford it, and you're not trying to sell the same songs as those you're giving away, it's worthwhile to give people a sample of your music. At the end of the gig, you might have quite a few postcards handed in. Copy out people's names and address onto a 'labels' A4 sheet (as for your press list), then mail people back a new postcard plus your free CD. You can use the previously filled-in cards for your first mailout by sticking new information over the old label, thus avoiding wasting cards.

If you have a website and the ability to send email mailshots, then it's much easier to build up a mailing list, by leaving forms to fill in at the merchandise desk and, most importantly, plugging this fact from the stage.

After a few gigs, you should have built up a small list of people who have been interested enough in the band to bother filling in the card. You can now market yourself to these people by selling them merchandise, gig tickets and new demos. If each of these people turn up at your next gig with a few mates, it's easy to imagine how your audience could snowball in size.

It's worth giving the people on your mailing list the chance to buy reduced-price tickets for your gigs to ensure that they turn up. Many promoters will see the sense in this and agree to allow in at a reduced fee anyone carrying a special flyer given to the people on the band's mailing list.

Always stress that it's free to join your 'Information Service', and plug it wherever possible. Bearing in mind that burning a three-song CD is unlikely to cost more than 50p, it's as well to give away at least some CDs – say, to the first 100 people who join the Information Service. In this way, at least some of the crowd at the next shows will know some of the songs.

Once the mailing list has reached a significant size, and you have started playing London shows, you may be able to fund coach trips for your fans to London at a reasonable price per head. Any London promoter will be more likely to give you a gig if he is guaranteed that you will bring some local supporters. If you're from a long way out of London, and your fans don't often travel to the capital, you need to be a bit devious in ensuring that they turn up to the gig. Sell them a gig ticket along with the coach ticket (not as part of the coach ticket – you'll have to give the gig-ticket part of the money to the promoter) and make sure that the pickup for the return coach trip is at the gig itself, so the fans have to turn up there rather than wander around Soho! If the coach is the right type, you might be able to fit your backline on board as well to save your own transport costs. Another idea is to run a joint coach trip between two bands who are appearing on the same bill.

# Merchandise

The only problem with merchandise is that it requires an immediate cash outlay to manufacture, say, T-shirts, before you can sell them. You should be able to get a small quantity – say 50 – good-quality white or black T-shirts made for around £4, all inclusive, depending on the complexity of, and colours contained in, your artwork. Most major cities and towns have T-shirt-printing firms, if you're not already aware of them. You should be looking for good-quality shirts – Hanes, Screen Stars or Fruit Of The Loom – with a striking design. Don't go mad with your first batch of shirts; stick to plain colours, or just black, with a fairly tasteful design incorporating the band's logo.

You'll need to give the T-shirt company a PMT or JPEG of your logo (or a very good photocopy) so they can make a silk screen, for which there'll be a charge (although, once made, you can use the screen in the future). Payment should be 50% upfront and 50% on collection.

There is a huge profit to be made on merchandise. Bands with a devoted live following have, over the years, survived on merchandising income long before they made much money from gigs or record sales. The average price of a T-shirt at a concert by a major artist is £18, but you should be selling yours for around the £12 mark; you need people to buy and wear them to promote the band, so profits should be secondary. Resist the temptation to get the cheapest T-shirts possible, however, as people would rather pay for a quality item that will last than something that will obviously fall to bits after a few months.

Although T-shirts are probably the standard item of merchandise, there are cheaper alternatives, such as badges, for those supporters who just want to part with £1 or so, and for this you can even buy your own badge-making machine! Badges are also cheap 'giveaway' promo items, as are stickers. If you check out the websites of major artists, or major merchandising companies such as Bravado (www.bravadolive.com), you will rapidly get an idea of the range of merchandise you could have to sell.

Keep a careful track of your merchandise stock, as it's all too easy to give away 20 shirts to mates, your family, other band's crew, etc. You should calculate your break-even point on your manufacturing costs and accept that you're going to have to give away a certain number of shirts.

# Compilation CDs

Many companies advertise for bands to send in recordings to appear on compilation CDs, which are then sent around the industry with the aim of creating some interest, although it has to be said that some unscrupulous companies charge bands a fortune to appear on bizarre compilations that only the most desperate A&R men would have in their offices.

Whilst I would not wish to tar all such companies with the same brush, I am not aware of any artist who has achieved any kind of meaningful recording or publishing deal directly through such exposure. However, some such compilations have played a part in bringing artists to the attention of the industry. In much the same way as a particular venue can develop a reputation for booking bands who go on to greater things, particular compilations will be taken more seriously in the A&R community if they have proved to be an interesting source of talent. If you find the idea of appearing on such a compilation appealing, I would simply urge caution when it comes to the cost. Remember the point about favoured nations (see Chapter 1) and ask the compilation company some tough questions about whether any of their compilations has ever led to anything.

Perhaps slightly more useful are compilations of local bands released in conjunction with a local newspaper or studio. At least with these the live audience in your area gets a chance to check out some bands they might not have been previously aware of, and might end up at one of your gigs.

# Stunts

There is no limit to the wild schemes dreamed up by bands and managers over the years in an attempt to bring themselves to the attention of the music business. They have ranged from the basic – graffiti and stickers spread around record companies' offices, or sweets with demo packages being sent to their entire A&R department – to the ambitious, where unsigned bands have pulled up outside record companies' offices playing on the back of a flatbed truck. On one memorable occasion, one band went as far as hiring the old Hammersmith Odeon – for a gig where 30 people turned up!

Nobody in the business minds stunts, as long as they don't inconvenience anyone or cost them any money, but equally well they may well end up doing the perpetrators more harm than good, in that they may make the industry take them less seriously. There is a frivolous side to the industry when organising promotional scams for their signed artists, but the idea that some kind of stunt is going to ensure a deal for a new band just displays a naivety that the industry will find off-putting.

Of far more use is staging newsworthy events for the local media, which will ensure that the band gets coverage for a gig or record release, such as giving away some kind of amusing item for the first 50 people through the door of a gig or making up some ridiculously implausible story about one of the band members. At least in this way your local profile will increase.

## A&R Magazines And Websites

There are several magazines and numerous websites advertised in the music press that supposedly offer inside information on the latest news and gossip from the world of A&R. Whilst the ones that charge money are not particularly expensive, I have found that certain of them seem to contain information that is of little use, or available free of charge elsewhere.

However, to be fair, it is often the case that the most insignificant snippet of information can be the factor that puts an artist on the track of a deal. In addition, general information about the industry, as well as gossip, is always going to be a useful part of any artist's arsenal. At the end of the day, there are masses of newspapers and magazines to which an aspiring artist could subscribe if the money was available, but if I had to select only one it would be *Music Week*.

# Gigs

Gigging is the traditional way to give any band exposure. By building up a live following, however small, you will be demonstrating to record companies, managers, agents and promoters that you may be worth their attention. Very few bands who have never gigged get record deals, and the world's most successful artists have always been those who are also great performers.

In major cities there are still plenty of pub and club gigs available for aspiring bands. In general, the only way to draw yourself to the attention of record companies and the national press is to play in cities or the larger towns, particularly London. Although record companies and press have staff in the regions, playing the London circuit may bring you to their attention earlier than they might otherwise notice you. There's no point in gigging until you're ready on two levels. Firstly, you need to be ready in terms of having a strong set, being well rehearsed and playing confidently. Secondly, you need to be ready on a business and administrative level in order to make the most of such gigs, using some of the tips contained earlier in this chapter.

If you play a bad gig, nobody who sees it will come and see you again readily. There's even less point in gigging in London until you're confident playing live and have done at least 20 local shows in order to find your feet.

# How To Get Local Gigs

Once you are rehearsed up with at least a 40-minute set, you need to gig locally in order to gain experience of performing live. Getting yourself gigs will be difficult unless you've previously been in local gigging bands, or you already have a guaranteed following.

The first thing to do is to make a list of local gigs – say, those within a ten-mile radius. Call each venue and ask for the name and address of the promoter. Ask how far ahead gigs are booked and whether or not the venue operates a 'new bands' night. Once you've established this, send off a package containing your demo, a photo and any press you have. Follow up with a call a week or so later, and only if you get offered a gig should you begin to discuss the deal on offer. Remember, promoters respect bands who they can see have put some effort into making the gig a success. If they can see flyers, a mailing list, posters, press and other types of self-publicity going on, they will look favourably on a band, assuming that they're musically interesting in the first place. Bands with a bad attitude, who have unreasonable demands and expectations, and who make little effort to promote their own gigs will be given short shrift.

# Payment For Gigs

There is no standard form of agreement for being paid for gigs. New bands who don't have a guaranteed audience have to take what they can get, although the Musicians' Union has, in recent years, mounted a vociferous campaign against 'pay to play' systems. Under such schemes, venues sell bands tickets for their own gigs, which the band then has to resell to its fans in order to make any money. In theory, some 'pay to play' systems can work out well if a band is confident enough of its ability to sell tickets and receives them sufficiently in advance of the gig.

Although in an ideal world everyone would be paid fairly for work of any kind, it's hard not to feel a lot of sympathy for small promoters, despite their somewhat chiselling demeanour. At heart, many club and pub promoters are idealists who love live music and get scant thanks from the local audience for their efforts. They are constantly told by bands that huge crowds of punters will descend on the night they play, only to be cruelly disappointed as the band (who are quite convinced that they are the next Oasis) play to a motley collection of their mums and dads.

The promoter also knows that, once the band go on to greater things, he will be passed over in favour of bigger promoters and his contribution totally forgotten.

The question you need to ask yourself is actually the same as the promoter is asking himself: Why would anyone pay to come and see you?

The deal you will be offered will fall into one of the following categories:

## (i) Fee

You will receive a 'guarantee' only, however many tickets the promoter sells. This arrangement is normal for 99% of all support bands and also for headline acts in small pubs and clubs;

## (ii) Guarantee Plus Split

You will receive a basic guarantee plus a percentage of the promoter's profits. Be careful to ensure that the contract sets out specifically what costs the promoter is allowed to deduct before he is in 'profit'. The highest split you are likely to get is 80% in your favour;

## (iii) Split Only

Accepting a split with no guarantee is fine if you are confident of your ability to pull paying punters. If you have no guarantee, however, try to ensure that the split is calculated on gross earnings. If you attract only small audiences, you're not in much of a bargaining position.

# Contracts With Promoters

Promoters of small pub and club gigs might not have any kind of contract with the bands they book, but others will have a standard agreement covering stage times and fees, including clauses that prevent the band from appearing within a certain number of miles from the gig for a period of time before it.

Some form of agreement is always desirable and a sample contract can be found in Appendix 8.

# Finding Out About The Gig

In your conversations with any promoter, you will need to find out:

•       The precise address of the gig, with directions, the phone number and a contact name to ask for on the day;

- Where you can park, whether parking is free, where the loading doors are, if there are any steps and what time you can get in;

- What the dimensions of the stage are and whether or not there are any drum risers;

- What time the PA is arriving, if it's not an in-house system;

- Details of the PA – its wattage, number of channels and type of effects and microphones, together with the address and number of the PA company, with a contact name;

- If there is any in-house backline and, if so, if the bands are expected to share it or share each other's backline;

- How many other bands are playing on your night and what the soundcheck times, door times and stage times are;

- What the contact details of the other bands are;

- Whether or not a rider (ie food and drink) will be provided;

- Is there a curfew (ie the latest time you can leave the premises)?

- Will the promoter be flyposting the local area or putting up posters in the club and/or taking press ads? If so, find out if he needs any more of your photos, posters or biogs, and ask if you can help out by contacting the local press;

- Does the venue have an area for selling merchandise? If so, will they provide somebody to sell your gear, and what percentage of your takings will they charge?

- Can you have a guest list – and, if so, for how many people?

- Does the promoter offer cheaper entry for those people carrying your flyers?

- Is there a dressing room for you, and is it lockable?

- Does the venue have its own lights, or will it be hiring them from outside? If so, what are their specifications, and is there an operator?

# Liaising With The Venue PA Or PA Company

It is extremely advisable to call the PA company or house sound engineer to introduce yourself. Establish how many crew they will be providing and be prepared to give them details of your backline, specifically potentially time-consuming set-ups such as an unusual number of DIs, a larger than average drum kit, multiple keyboards and the like.

Be prepared to send the PA company a stage plan, however rough, showing the preferred position of your backline, describing each item and paying particular attention to the vocal set-up. The plan should also have your input list and monitor-mix requirements. It's a good idea to post this information on your website so that, if you are in email contact with them, you can simply send them the link.

If you can talk directly to the person who will be mixing the sound on the night, and he or she seems receptive, you could send them a demo and/or invite them to a prior gig. Many sound engineers like getting involved at the early stages of a band's career if they can see that the band has potential, although it has to be said that some club and small independent PA companies' engineers are the wrong side of deaf and cynical!

# Rehearsals

Every band needs to rehearse, and it's important to get the most out of each rehearsal session. Although cost is always an issue, it really is better to rehearse at a professional facility with an adequate PA and perhaps some backline, which you can hire to save transport hassles. Always record each rehearsal; at the very least, it will save time at the next rehearsal while the band members try to remember what they did last time.

It almost goes without saying that everyone needs to turn up on time and with a clear idea of what needs to be achieved at each rehearsal – for example, learning a new song, or trying the live set in a different order, or trying new arrangements. It's also important for every member of the band – particularly the writers – to be open-minded and allow the band to try out different ideas. One common reason for people leaving bands is that they feel their contributions are being overlooked or not appreciated.

If your budget can stand it, storing your own gear at the same facility you rehearse at will save a lot of hassle, and will also provide the band with a 'hub' to meet up at. The bigger rehearsal facilities – certainly in London – are also a mine of useful industry contacts, gossip and opportunities.

# On Stage

If a band is inexperienced at performing live, then every gig can teeter on the brink of disaster until they start to play regularly. However, there are areas that, given some attention, can reduce the possibility of embarrassment.

- The first is general organisation, meaning that everyone needs to turn up in good time, with everything they need. If one member of the band is constantly pissing the others off by being late and untogether, then the rest have to ask themselves if it's worth putting up with that kind of bad attitude.

- The band needs to delegate various jobs – such as copying out set lists, sorting out the guest list and so on – amongst themselves. Most importantly, at load-out, someone (perhaps the band member delegated with staying sober and driving) needs to do a final check of the dressing rooms and stage to ensure that nothing has been left behind.

- Mark all your gear with the band's name and a contact number, and try to put the band's name on the bass drum skin.

- Don't turn the soundcheck into a jam session. Explain clearly what everyone needs in their monitors and then play through as many songs as possible.

- The set needs to be timed to within a minute or so. Over-running will incur the wrath of the promoter and the other bands on the bill, and finishing unexpectedly early may mean that there's a huge gap before the next band comes onto the stage. Worst of all, the band will appear unprofessional and disorganised.

- It's common sense, but you need to tune up five minutes before going on stage. A guitar left on a stage under hot lights will detune very quickly.

- Every band member needs to have a spare to cover every eventuality, from a spare snare through to spare guitars and strings. If the gig is an important one – and every gig should be – then a mate at the side of the stage tuning the guitars is a luxury that may be worth paying for.

- If someone screws up, don't all turn and stare at them, and only ever stop a song in the event of a total disaster. Remember that the audience might not even have noticed a mistake.

- It doesn't matter if there are only 20 people at the gig. It's not their fault that nobody else turned up. You should give them the same energy and commitment that you would give to a capacity crowd.

- Don't make excuses from the stage – ie 'We can't hear anything up here' – because nobody in the audience cares or understands what technical hitches are happening. There's nothing worse than hearing a band slag off a monitor engineer or front-of-house engineer instead of just asking firmly for a few changes to be made.

- Whoever the frontperson is, work on the patter between songs, and have something in reserve in case anything goes wrong. Always be ready to plug forthcoming gigs and your mailing list. Work the set around the guitar changes, keep the energy up, and don't stop after every song.

- Buy the sound guy a drink.

- Tell the audience who you are, at the start and at the end of the set. And during it!

- Plug your website.

- Leave them wanting more.

Once the organisational and technical side has settled down, turn your attention to showmanship, stage presence and confidence. Concentrate on giving the audience a great night out, do your thing and don't appear embarrassed to be there. Even the reserved British quietly appreciate a bit of good old-fashioned swagger, so take yourself seriously and everyone else will begin to as well. That doesn't mean shuffling onto the stage dressed like a bunch of plumbers and mumbling to yourselves. Take the show to the crowd.

# Gig Etiquette

Promoting at pub and club levels is a risky business that tends to attract no-nonsense individuals who have no patience with bands who are unprofessional, arrogant or difficult to work with. Be courteous to the promoter, adhere to your stage and soundcheck times and use common sense – for example, don't assume that you'll be able to walk in and out of the gig all night; ask if there are passes. Remember that all local promoters talk to each other, and you need to leave a good impression. Don't assume that you can have an unlimited guest list and suddenly spring another ten names on the promoter, or that you can have a few free beers. If the attendance is a disaster, don't imply that this is the promoter's fault; remember that, whatever money you might have spent in staging the gig, the promoter has undoubtedly lost more.

At the end of the night, ask about a return booking, and always make sure that the promoter has your phone number or, preferably, business card. Make a mental note of forthcoming gigs at the venue and ask specifically if you can support certain bands that you feel you fit with, musically.

## Supporting Other Bands

If you get the chance to support a signed band, or any band with their own production (ie PA and lights), remember that it is their gig and their name on the ticket. Don't assume that you'll be able to use their PA and lights without paying their crew to work during your set, and expect minimal stage room and no monitors. Don't expect to be allowed to use the headliner's gear – even a single DI box – or to be able to sell your merchandise on their stand.

After establishing all the necessary gig information as if it's your own gig, turn up in good time and set up your backline in the hall, ready to be loaded onto the stage as soon as the main band have finished soundchecking. The promoter will probably be busy making sure that the headliners are happy and that the door times are going to be met, so introduce yourself to the band's tour manager or production manager and then stay out of the way.

Whatever the promoter has agreed about the number of channels you'll get, the room on stage and who will be doing your sound, you can bet that this won't have been communicated to the headliners' crew. More often than not, if they are in mid-tour, they will be totally knackered and looking forward to a pre-show meal, and a support band pestering them is likely to be met with extreme annoyance.

Money (or a few free T-shirts) goes a long way to smoothing the waters, and perhaps the headliners' monitor man will agree to mix your front-of-house sound, if only to ensure that the headliners' settings are left alone. Stay out of the way of the headline band unless they seem particularly friendly, and don't blunder in and out of their dressing room unannounced. If they are receptive, and have perhaps watched your set, give them a demo or some T-shirts and you might get the chance to support them in the future.

# The Big Move To London

Sooner or later, every artist or band from the regions of the UK begins to give thought to the idea of moving to London. There is no doubt that, whilst many cities and towns in the UK have a thriving music scene and a scattering of small labels, the UK's music industry is almost entirely centred in London. If I had to give a 'yes' or 'no' answer as to whether moving to London is necessary or a good idea, it would be a resounding 'yes', qualified with 'and probably the sooner the better'.

Many bands spend years languishing in the regions, gradually building a local following and perhaps playing the odd gig in London. People get older, get permanent jobs and relationships and all of a sudden a complete change of environment seems much more of a risk than it did when everyone had just left college or was still in their teens. There is no doubt that making a move to London to have a serious attempt at making it in the industry is a big commitment, and it is a rare band whose members are all completely of one mind about it. Some will be living at home, others will have jobs, some will have some money, others will be completely broke. It's a big one.

A great band I know started life in just about the most desolate town in the UK, and after a while they all decided to move to London. They literally packed all their gear and possessions into a van, and after one of them had spent a week or two in London dossing on a mate's couch whilst finding a house to rent, they made the move. Within a week, all of them had jobs – some working behind a bar, others doing cycle courier work and a bit of cash-in-hand – and spent the rest of their time hassling for gigs. They got gigs because they had a great demo and also had enough front to pester people to come and pay to see them, so they got rebooked. Now, they spray paint or sticker their logo wherever they go. They blag studio time and blag their way into other bands' gigs. They haven't moved to London for a laugh; they've moved down to get the industry talking about them – and it's working. They've now had two singles out on a small, poverty-stricken indie label and a couple of sessions on Xfm. People are starting to take notice.

The point of this example – and where this band are succeeding, thousands have failed or given up – is that this band are using London to their own ends and not being overawed by the idea of a move to 'the big Smoke'. They are all young enough so that, if it doesn't happen for them, there is plenty of time for them to do something else with their lives. If this band falls apart, then I guess some of them may go back home and some of them may join other bands. (Incidentally, from what I have seen, the band have certainly bonded together as a result of this shared adventure, from living in the same house and rehearsing and writing together regularly.)

There are many misconceptions about life in London. Yes, rent is much more expensive than anywhere else in the UK, but there are still cheap places to be found. You don't have to traipse round looking for somewhere to rent, like you would have had to a few years ago; you can find places online instead. Rehearsal rooms are a bit more expensive, but the people you meet there are a lot more useful than those you might meet in rehearsal rooms anywhere else. Going out costs more, unless you know where to go. Taxis are ridiculously expensive, but the Tube isn't as bad as it is made out to be. Studios in London are more expensive, but it's easier to blag free time in them. Pub and club gigs are better there than anywhere else, and there is a much higher chance that industry people will be there. The city seems enormous, but it is manageable. And, contrary to popular belief, there are many jobs to be found in London.

There is probably no point, however, in moving to London without a distinct plan and goals, an initial budget to rent somewhere and a commitment to at least give it a year. For a solo artist, as opposed to a band, it can be a daunting idea to move to a strange city and begin slogging around the clubs or trying to put a band together. If you're a member of a band, solo artist or manager based in the regions, I think the real question is this: If you don't make it in the business, will you spend years afterwards wondering if there was something you could have done – such as moving to London – that would have made all the difference?

To be really blunt, if you're in a band and most of you want to move to London and have a serious go at making it, then get rid of the ones who really don't.

# CHAPTER 7

# AGENTS, PROMOTERS AND TOURS

Many people outside the music industry get confused about the difference between managers, agents and promoters. Showbusiness stars tend to refer to their representatives as their 'agents' when in fact these people could be performing the functions of a manager, or indeed a press agent. In the music industry, the demarcation between these roles is a lot clearer.

# Agents

Finding an agent is a vital step forward for any new band. To have somebody to take over the hassle of getting you gigs, and who believes in you at a very early stage, is extremely welcome.

## What Do Agents Do?

An agent's function is to get his bands as many gigs as possible and to help the band put together a sensible gigging strategy. Agents are in constant touch with promoters throughout the UK and with other agents who exchange information about which of their bands are touring and may need an opening act, or which might want to open up for another band. An agent will work closely with a band's management and record company at all times, keeping in constant touch to ensure that the band are ready to gig if an opportunity arises.

There are relatively few agents in the UK, but the major players wield enormous influence in the music business. If you're signed to a major agency at an early stage, that agent's roster of other bands opens up enormous touring opportunities for you.

Once a gigging strategy is established and a tour is booked, it is the agent's job to make sure that all parties, from the band to the manager and the promoter, work well together and make the tour a success. This will encompass everything from making sure the tour is being advertised properly to ensuring that the promoter is getting co-operation from the management and vice versa – liaising with the tour manager on occasion – and, perhaps most importantly, ensuring that the band is getting paid!

# How To Find An Agent

It is extremely difficult for a new band to find an agent immediately, unless they have a serious manager already on board who will have convinced several agents that they are the next big thing. The reality is that agents need to pay their bills, and booking a new band into a few £50 gigs every month isn't going to generate enough commission even to cover the agent's phone calls.

However, if a band is starting to attract some attention on a local level and is pulling good crowds, it is likely that their name will have been mentioned in passing to a few agents by local promoters. The reason for this is that the agent might have an established act playing in that venue in the near future but be concerned that the attendance might not be as good as it could be. The obvious solution is to offer a support slot to a local band who will pull that extra 30 or 40 people needed to make the gig a success. Even if the show is part of a tour with a support act doing the whole tour, it is extremely common to use a local band as third on the bill, or 'first on', to get people into the gig early and drinking at the bar. Hopefully, the agent will actually turn up to the gig early enough to see your band, although it has to be said that most agents don't tend to travel far outside London unless it's to see their major clients.

Many bands are somewhat disgruntled about doing a 'first on' set just after the doors have opened, but there are some upsides: the chance to play to new people; soundchecking last so that at least your monitors are good for your set; the chance to 'nick' the main band's audience; and, not least, the chance to flyer the gig and hopefully sell some merchandise.

Most of the major agencies have websites listing who their clients are, and even if they don't then a bit of research through album credits should reveal who your favourite bands' agents are. You should have a strong idea of which bands, at your level, would be ideal for you to support if they played in your town or city (be realistic). It's not beyond the realms of possibility that, if you send their agent a demo asking for a support slot next time they play in your area, you might get a call.

# Agents' Fees

Agents, rather like managers, make their money by charging a percentage – in their case, a percentage of the fees paid to their bands for gigs. The standard agent's commission is between 10% and 15% of the artist's gross earnings. For major artists able to command guarantees of hundreds of thousands of dollars per night, their agents will commission at a much lower rate. The contract an artist would be expected to sign with an agent will be relatively short and straightforward; however, many major bands have not had any kind of formal written arrangements with their agents until the Government recently changed the regulations relating to employment agencies.

Here's short list of things you should be aware of:

- You will probably be expected to sign with the agent worldwide. You should check what arrangements he has with agents in other territories, particularly the USA, in order to ensure that you don't end up paying commission twice;

- The contract is unlikely to be for less than five years. In practice, agents are more willing than, say, record companies or managers to allow you to move elsewhere if the relationship is not working;

- The commission may reduce on fees over and above a set level;

- The agent will send you a bill for his fees quarterly or half-yearly.

# Promoters

You'll begin dealing with local promoters almost as soon as you begin gigging. At a pub and club level, they are almost always the nervous and depressed-looking individual who is hovering around the door. A promoter is, in essence, anyone who stages a public event and charges admission to that event. Promoters make their money by staging events for which the costs are less than the income received from ticket sales, plus income from other areas such as merchandising, sponsorship, etc. Promoting is a high-risk operation and there are only a small number of major promoters in the UK, who finance and stage entire tours as well as one-off events and festivals. Whichever major venue you attend, you'll see the names of Clearchannel, SJM and Metropolis – to name just a few – on your ticket.

It's always interesting to try to work out the economics of any show you may be attending, in order to develop an understanding of the amounts of money that are available to a touring band. You will rapidly be able to guess how many people are in a room (if you're a manager, the real number is, of course, half the number you told everyone), then take the ticket price, knock off the VAT, multiply it by the number of people in the audience, knock off some guests and arrive roughly at the amount of money in the room. It's usually less than you might imagine!

## Agents Contracting With Promoters

It's important to note that, once you have an agent working for you, it's the agent who will prepare the contract with a promoter on your behalf. You will already have advised him of details such as your rider, PA and lighting requirements, and he will have negotiated the guarantee/percentage with the promoter and all other aspects of the deal. The contract will then be forwarded by your agent to you and the promoter for signature. Your agent will not sign it.

Most agencies issue standard contracts, and in the case of major artists, these can be incredibly detailed when it comes to the rider. Contrary to popular belief, the rider does not simply specify that all brown M&Ms will be removed from each bowl before the band will deign to play the show, but covers every last aspect of what is required from the promoter, ranging from catering to production, through to restrictions on filming and so on.

It's always amusing to read stories in the press about the supposedly 'outrageous demands' of major artists. Usually, on closer examination, these turn out to be 'demands' for such luxuries as food, a clean toilet and perhaps some seats. The reality for a major artist on tour is that, by the time the first few shows are out of the way and any technical or creative glitches are ironed out, the tour should roll like a well-oiled machine and deliver the best possible experience to the paying punters. This goal can be achieved only if the promoters in each territory understand what the tour's requirements are and stick to them, or be taken to task by the tour manager or production manager if they haven't complied with the requirements of the artist. The alternative might be that there is nowhere arranged for the trucks to park, the stage can't take the weight of the backline, everybody is wandering around with the wrong passes on, and that night's show will be a nightmare.

# Touring

Once a band is signed to a record company, it is critical that every gig done after that maximises the band's profile. It is extremely common, therefore, for record companies to advance bands the money they need to upgrade their gear (as set out in the record deal) as part of an overall 'tour support' budget. A band that has only ever been playing at pub and club level is unlikely to have the correct gear if the chance of a City Hall/Apollos tour supporting a major band comes up, and it's better to invest in new, properly flightcased and insured gear than to waste money on hired equipment.

'Tour support' is an oft-used expression and means simply that a band's record company (or, more unusually, their publishing company) is funding the loss on a tour. In all cases, tour support is treated as an extra advance and is therefore recoupable against the band. These days, record companies are beginning to demand shares of bands' merchandising and PRS income in order to lessen tour support bills.

Many signed bands – and you may be salivating at this point – get free or reduced-price equipment from suppliers in return for endorsing their product. The reduced-price deal will usually be the 'trade' price of the gear, which means around half price. No major signed band would pay anything for guitar strings and drum heads; they are given away free by the manufacturers in almost all cases.

You may have heard of something called a 'buy-on'. This is a sum of money paid by a support band to a headline band for the privilege of supporting them. This practice is rife and has come about largely due to the ever-increasing costs of touring – as well as an unhealthy dose of greed amongst bigger bands.

The logic from the headliner's point of view is that they are giving the opening band access to a much larger audience than they could command on their own, as well as allowing the support acts to use their PA and lights. The best that the support band can do in these situations is to get the most value for their money as possible by agreeing in writing that they will be given a set number of channels on the desk, adequate monitors, follow spots, catering, free trucking, their merchandise sold by the headliners' crew – in fact, anything and everything that will help to claw back some of the buy-on costs. If a solo artist goes on a UK arena tour with a hired band and an 'average' buy-on, it wouldn't be unusual for the total tour support/buy-on bill to exceed £50,000.

# CHAPTER 8

# RELEASING YOUR OWN RECORD

## Motivation

There's a world of difference between pressing up 1,000 singles from your demo and actually releasing an indie single on a real label, however small.

Making your own record is an expensive but relatively straightforward business. However, it's important to analyse your reasons for choosing this option. It's important not to go into this as a kind of ego trip, because it's hard to maintain a big ego whilst looking at hundreds of unsold CDs gathering dust in your garage. Anyone with some money can call themselves Wibble Records (or whatever) and get a record pressed. If your record isn't nationally distributed, and not reviewed, then effectively it is not being 'released' in the traditional sense. Could the money involved be better spent on studio or rehearsal time, or new gear, or on London gigs? If you're releasing your own record because of years of rejection by the music industry, is it possible that your songs are, in fact, rubbish?

Before you go to the time, trouble and expense of making and releasing your own record, you need to be extremely clear about what your goals are. You must analyse how many people might actually buy your record, either at gigs, via your website or perhaps via some low-level national distribution. You need to decide how many copies you'll need to use for promotional purposes, such as press reviews and radio play, and how many you'll need to give away free to friends and family.

For most artists, having some kind of independent release – whether it is a single, an EP, a mini album or a full album – is a very traditional early step in their career. Despite the fact that this is not likely to be a profitable exercise, the benefits of raising the artist's profile may be far greater than the cost and hard work involved.

It may be that a small independent label takes an interest in a band and is prepared to fund the release of a single or mini-album. This is unlikely to happen without the band having already built up some kind of profile and without having to commit to a long-term contract. It would be extremely unusual to find a philanthropic, well-funded label prepared to stump up the money to release a one-off piece of product and then lose the band to another label if the release paid off.

So, for the purpose of this chapter I will assume that a band wishes to release its own product, on its own 'label', and examine the mechanics of doing so.

# Recordings

Assuming that the band has some well-recorded demo tracks, it is likely that one track in particular will be standing out as a strong song, both from the band's point of view and in terms of the reaction from friends and audiences. Provided that the band hasn't already exhausted the possibilities of this track by selling it at gigs, making it available for downloads, having it reviewed in the local press and so on, it's likely that it should be the lead track of a single release, which would also feature one or two other tracks.

If there are a larger number of recordings, with numerous strong tracks, it may be more sensible to consider releasing a five- or six-track mini-album instead.

On balance, most early releases by established acts have tended to be singles for a number of reasons, including:

• The possibility of radio play;

• Having a 'signature' track that encapsulates everything the band is about at that moment;

- Cost of recording, mastering and manufacture;

- Lower selling price;

- The possibility of press reviews.

We should therefore proceed on the basis that the band in question is going to release an independent single, with a lead track and two other tracks. The first thing to deal with is the actual recordings that will appear on it.

# Mastering

The first stage in the process is to have the recordings properly mastered and to finalise the running order of the single. Clearly the lead track will be first, but you might decide that the keys or tempos of the other two tracks lend themselves to appearing in a different order than you might have imagined.

Professional mastering facilities tend to cost between £50 and £150 per hour, plus the cost of any copies and, of course, VAT. During the mastering process, the depth, clarity and compression of the recordings can be dramatically altered: hiss and hum can be removed, sibilance toned down and EQ added. To a certain extent, tracks can be sped up or slowed down, and fades on tracks can be cleaned up and lengthened or shortened.

You should aim to meet up with a mastering engineer before the session starts, and be sure to play him any records by other bands that have the sonic qualities you're looking for. Despite the fact that they may have been recorded in a £1,500-per-day studio, your tracks may be able to get into the same ballpark, in terms of quality, once they are mastered, if the original recordings are good enough. Bear in mind, however, that at most mastering facilities you're hearing things through speakers that may cost more than a small car!

For the sake of argument, mastering a three-track single might take up to 90 minutes (in which case, find out if the studio charges for two hours) including copying time. It's best if the whole band attends the session in order to avoid arguments afterwards, but only if this won't mean wasting time on long discussions while the clock is ticking (the running order should certainly be decided before the session starts, for example). At the end of it, you should have a master CDR and a safety copy of your single, plus a couple of copies.

# The Label

Before moving on to deal with artwork, we need to digress and deal with the actual 'label' that will release the single. It's much better if the band don't appear to be releasing the single on their own label, but instead on some seemingly unconnected label that has apparently signed the band. This is for the simple reason that it may seem slightly sad for the band to have had to have gone to the lengths of releasing their own record, as it appears that nobody else is prepared to do so. Some subterfuge is therefore required. Also, quite aside from this, it's no bad thing for a band to treat its label as a quite separate project.

In an ideal world, the label would have its own website and also appear to be releasing product by other artists. It would have its own headed paper, a different address to that of the band (even if this is a PO box number) and people other than the band working for it (even if these people were actually the band using different email addresses). With a bit of lateral thinking and a certain amount of money, a plausible-looking 'front' label can be created which, to the world at large, is releasing the single.

Actually creating the label need amount to little more than checking that the suggested name isn't being used elsewhere, registering the domain name (if possible) and designing a simple logo. In reality, the label is no more than a 'trading style' of the band, and if payments need to be made to the label – for example, by people buying the single online or payments from a distributor – then it will be relatively straightforward to open a bank account linked to the main band account, in the name of the label, or to agree with the bank that cheques payable to the label can be credited to the band's account.

Ideally, the band's website would link to the label's site, both for sales of CDs and for business enquiries. It's not unusual – particularly if a band is in a very distinct musical genre – to get licensing enquiries from overseas labels if a single is attracting good reviews in the UK and online (see later).

Whether or not there is a label website, at the very least the label must have the following:

- Headed paper and a plausible postal address, email address and phone number;

- A memorable name and logo;

- A label band biography;

- A label press release for the single.

# Distribution

Moving on – and right now all we have is a mastered CDR of the single – all labels have some form of distribution. So what is distribution?

Essentially, distribution is what the word implies: the process by which the label gets its product sold and delivered into the shops, and sold through other channels such as online. Major labels tend either to have their own distribution companies or to use the larger independent distributors, all of which carry tens of thousands of lines of products, employ large sales forces and have gigantic warehouses brimming with CDs, DVDs and numerous other formats.

Aside from the major distributors, there are dozens of much smaller operations that tend to focus more on specific genres of music, whether it be techno, folk or punk. Many are run by no more than three or four people but use a major distributor to store their product physically and fulfil sales orders. These smaller distributors are your target in your attempt to get your single distributed.

It may seem far-fetched that a single by an unknown band would attract the attention of a distributor, but it is by no means impossible. By reading *Music Week*, and being aware of the names of distributors who seem to deal in releases by bands in your genre, you can pinpoint those companies who are most closely allied with your type of music. A bit of research will reveal their addresses and the names of the 'label managers' at each distributor.

Any distributor, whatever the merits of the product they are offered, will simply focus on how many sales are likely to be achieved, and on what marketing and promotion the 'label' will be doing to make this as likely as possible. For example, if you're in a hardcore punk band, the distributor may already know that they can shift a couple of hundred copies of any single in this genre on export to Japan. If the *NME* has already reviewed a previous single favourably, again, the distributor will know that this is worth some sales of a new single. If the band has a ten-date support tour scheduled and a large mailing list, and the label can afford to take out an ad in The Fly, this is extremely encouraging.

There is no doubt that independent record retailers are having an extremely tough time, and there has to be a good reason for them to stock product by new bands. Similarly, the major multiple retailers will take product only if there are unassailable reasons for doing so ('They're supporting The Strokes on their UK tour' would be a good one). This not to say that people won't be able to order your single from these shops through the distributor, but it will almost certainly not be there in the record racks. It's likely, however, that it will be available through online retailers, as with every other piece of product that is distributed by that distributor.

Distributors make their money by charging a percentage of the price they receive from whoever they've sold their product to. This percentage is usually between 15% and 25%, and for an unknown band and label it will be at the highest end of this range. Some distributors will front the manufacturing cost of product (known as a 'pressing and distribution' deal) and then knock off the manufacturing costs from any income they're going to pass on to the label. It goes without saying that they're unlikely to take this risk on a new band and label.

Distribution agreements tend to be fairly standard and, although they should be negotiated by a solicitor acting on the band's or label's behalf, it may not be worth going to town and incurring legal costs on negotiating clauses that the distributor is loath to change. The agreement will deal with the percentages that the distributor wants to charge for a variety of types of sales, the territory, payment provisions, reserves against returns, etc.

It is therefore incorrect to assume that it's impossible for your first single release to achieve national and international distribution, be available on Amazon, and so on. It's simply a case of finding the right distributor, and for that distributor to have confidence that enough copies will be sold to make it a worthwhile exercise. A list of distributors can be found in Appendix 13.

# Artwork And Manufacturing

It's impossible to generalise about artwork, other than to remark that the artwork for any artist's first release should ideally be memorable, striking and stylish. Often, the genre of music will lend itself to a certain style of artwork, and all artists will have strong ideas not only about the way they wish to present themselves but also about the artwork produced by other artists that they like. It is very important that you don't use images or designs on artwork that may infringe copyright, and it's never a particularly good idea to use offensive imagery (at least, if you want retailers to stock the product).

Technical delivery requirements for artwork will vary depending on your choice of manufacturer, and it's vital to establish these requirements at the outset. It's also very important – if the product is to be properly distributed – to establish who will deal with the barcode for the release (usually the distributor).

If there is nobody within the band who feels that they can design the sleeve, it's usually possible to find a local designer who will put something together relatively cheaply, and often manufacturers and distributors have in-house design people whose services can be added to your bill.

Almost all distributors will have favoured manufacturers, and some may even be part of the same company; even if you've managed to find a slightly cheaper alternative manufacturer, it might involve considerably less hassle to use the distributor's recommendation.

Remember that, for an 'average' single release, you'll need to hold back several hundred copies for promotional purposes, whether they are for press reviews, radio stations, general industry promotions, or freebies. This will obviously raise the break-even point for the single, and it's as well to err on the side of generosity when it comes to deciding how many promo copies you'll need. It's likely that your distributor won't be based around the corner, and if you don't order enough you'll probably only end up paying extra to have a couple of urgently needed boxes of stock sent back to you. All distributors will be aware that any band will be selling copies of the single at gigs, but if you have a large following in a town or city with independent record shops, remember that this is only going to discourage them from stocking more than a few copies of the single.

It's important that you adhere to the MCPS's requirements when releasing your own record – in short, by making payments to the publisher(s) and therefore the writer(s) of the songs on your releases. The rate to factor into your budget is 8.5% of the published dealer price of your release, divided by the number of songs on it. You will usually have to pay the MCPS the full amount upfront, regardless of whether all the copies of the release get sold, in order for them to issue the mechanical licence necessary for the record to get pressed. You will, however, be able to manufacture a certain number of copies royalty-free as promotional stock intended to be given away, and the relevant forms can be obtained from the MCPS. If the songs are written by the band and aren't published by a music publisher, then you won't have to pay mechanical royalty payments and will be issued with a 'notice of no claim' by the MCPS on request. You might be required to show this to your manufacturer to prove that no royalties are payable.

# Scheduling

To be glib, everything usually takes twice as long as you imagined. If you wanted to release a single on 1 May (ie you wanted your distributor to schedule the release that week) it would have to be mastered by the end of January and the artwork ready by the middle of February, including the catalogue number and the barcode. Manufacturing might take a month, so by the middle of March you'd have your promo copies ready. Initial marketing and promotion should come in at this point.

Press reviews might start coming in by early to mid-April, which is the period during which your distributor will be trying to sell in the single to retailers, and you might begin to get radio play at the same time. The band should be playing dates throughout April and May, which will have needed to be booked in January or even December of the previous year.

As you can see, it's a long process and one that's prone to unexpected hiccups – artwork having glitches, delays on manufacturing and so on. Major labels can achieve incredibly fast turnarounds on releases by major artists, but in the real world months, rather than weeks, is the order of the day.

Release dates often get moved, but rarely by more than a few weeks, and people in the media are quite used to this. If you're expecting a review and a particular journalist isn't confirming a review because they seem to think that their review will be out of date by the time it gets printed, there's no harm in 'massaging' the actual release date in order to get the review.

One important factor is that, during the months of November and December, the entire music industry – from major labels through to distributors and the media – is entirely focused on the Christmas sales period. It is the worst possible time to introduce any brand-new artist, especially on their first release. There is a huge glut of material from established artists and compilation albums in the shops. Review space is tight, regular punters don't show up for gigs, and key industry people whose attention you're trying to attract are either caught up in a blizzard of dinners and parties or working around the clock to sell as many records as possible. Conversely, beginning in late January, the industry wakes up to the fact that a new year is upon it, settles down and becomes open to more new business.

Once you've assessed these factors, you'll be able to put together a very rough budget of income and expenditure, right down to the number of Jiffy bags you'll need and postage costs. It will rapidly become apparent that it is highly unlikely that a limited run of CD singles will produce any profit, and the break-even point for a limited number of albums will be several hundred sales at the very least.

The reality for any band or small label aiming for its first release is that precise budgeting and long-term planning, coupled with realism, are absolutely vital.

# Marketing And Promotion

The purpose of marketing and promotion is simply to raise awareness of a release, and therefore the artist, and thus to build an audience and sell as many copies of the release as possible. The idea is that your release will arrive on the shelves amid a flurry of activity that will drive people inexorably towards the cash registers. You will have seen that, for a major record company release by a priority artist, it's almost impossible to get away from the relentless marketing machine. The record seems to be on every radio station and advertised on every TV channel, the video is everywhere, pop-ups infest your computer screen, The Sun seems to run a story about the artist every day, massive tour dates are announced, and huge billboards appear in every city. Clearly, this kind of activity costs hundreds of thousands of pounds a week and is designed to propel key releases straight in at Number One, with opening-week sales of at least 100,000 units.

The bottom line with marketing any release by a new band on its own label is the question 'How much money have you got?' Depressing, I know. All new bands dream of full-page ads in The Fly and NME, great reviews in Uncut, videos screened on MTV2 and their music played on the radio. All of these things cost money: it costs money to book ads, and it costs money to pay for radio pluggers and press people.

It's not an entirely bleak picture, so if you have very little money, it's best to be realistic about what can be achieved and to be prepared to put in a lot of hard work yourself, instead of forking out for highly paid industry professionals to do it for you. It's as well to be aware that a radio plugger is unlikely to agree to plug a single to national radio for less than an upfront payment of £1,000 plus monthly retainers. Any press person will charge about the same. Unless you have this kind of money, you need to lower your expectations and look at replicating as much of the work of the pros as you can.

## Radio

An industry colleague of mine once memorably described radio pluggers as 'people you may huge amounts of money to tell you that nobody likes the record'. Harsh, but true. Professional radio pluggers make a living by getting records played, which means that they develop incredibly close contacts with all radio producers, DJs, session bookers and so on. Usually, they will know whether they stand any chance of getting a record played within a few minutes of hearing it and learning the plan surrounding its release.

So what radio play can you expect without a plugger? Very little, is the short answer. However, depending on your outfit's musical genre, there are key shows broadcast by stations such as Radio 1, Xfm and 6 Music that will play new music, as well as those of numerous online broadcasters who are more receptive to new artists. It may be that a local station will give your record the occasional spin if there is a buzz developing about the band amongst their audience. The key is research, which needs to be done months in advance of the release date.

If you develop a target list of DJs and producers for your release, then the approach needs to be made as the 'label', not as the band itself. You might even go as far as to dream up a fictional plugging company, allied to the label, and make your approach using that entity instead. However, there is no substitute for the direct personal contact favoured by professional pluggers. Some renowned plugging companies have developed much cheaper subsidiary companies that will plug releases by new artists to a limited selection of media. Again, research is the key, so if you take a look at the websites of some up-and-coming artists in a similar genre, very often they will have a section on their website detailing who their press and radio people are.

There are also numerous radio promotion people and companies that deal with regional radio and student radio, and it might be within your budget to get your release included in their regular mailouts.

## Press

In Chapter 6, 'Self-promotion And Gigs', you will have read the basic ground rules of handling press, most of which apply to releasing your own record.

Reviews and editorial coverage in the local and national press, as well as on the more credible websites, have the enormous merit of being effectively free of charge, apart from postage and phone calls. Again, planning is absolutely crucial. Months ahead of your release date, you need to build up a list of contacts at all magazines, newspapers and websites that you feel stand a good chance of reviewing your release. Unfortunately, there is no substitute for spending hours or even days on the phone, calling around to establish who the right people are. In the case of websites, it's often extremely difficult to establish their postal address, so you'll need to email them to find out what it is.

Initially, you need to establish who the reviews editor is at each organisation. All major publications have a person whose job it is to farm out review copies of releases to in-house and freelance journalists. Smaller magazine and websites will usually have everything being done by one or two people. The approach should be made using the 'label' identity you've created.

You need to establish each publication or webite's deadline for reviews, which, in the case of monthly magazines, may be at least two months before the actual 'street date' of the magazine. In addition, many publications will need a couple of copies of the release and perhaps a JPEG of the inlay card. The only way to deal with the dozens of publications and websites you intend to approach is to be totally methodical, by building up a spreadsheet of names, addresses, email and website addresses, deadlines and requirements. Unless you do this, even your mailouts will become the stuff of nightmares and disorganisation will cost you reviews.

Although it's tempting to imagine great reviews in the *NME*, *Q*, *Mojo* and so on, these major publications are inundated with product, and many of the monthly magazines don't review singles at all. However obscure a website may be, it is heartening to read a great review of your release anywhere, and if there's a fantastic quote in the review, you may end up using it on your biography or future press releases for months or even years to come.

Quite aside from reviews of specific product, there are numerous publications and websites that have a 'Ones To Watch'-type feature for new artists. If you want to be featured in there, you'll need to establish who edits that particular section and pitch the band to them. If the band has a series of dates coming up, and has already earned some encouraging early reviews, there is all the more reason for you to be considered for a feature.

Press officers and PR companies have unrivalled contacts amongst the frontline of music journalists and will also be able to deliver reviews in national newspapers, and, as with radio pluggers, some of these will offer low-priced schemes for new and impoverished artists. There are also press companies that deal exclusively with student press, fanzines and regional publications. Even allowing for this, most companies would expect a fee of between £500 and £1,000 for even the most basic workmanlike job on a new release.

## Promo Copies

Although most journalists, radio producers and others in the media are used to receiving advance promo copies of new singles and albums on CDR with basic inlay card details, it is better to send them finished product if you can. This will mean having your stock of finished CDs at least two months before the actual release date.

If you need to send advance promo copies to publications that have a very long lead time, it's very important to include the catalogue number of the release on the inlay card, together with the track listing (you don't necessarily need to include any tracks other than the lead track), the release date, and contact information for the 'label' and PR contact.

## Making A Video

Depending on the capabilities of your website, you might be able to get extremely creative by making videos and short films featuring the band and posting them up on the site.

However, unless you feel that you can create a video with some artistic merit, it's really better not to bother. Don't get conned into paying to have one of your gigs recorded on one or more Hi-8 or DV camcorders; the lighting is bound to be completely inadequate and the sound, taken from the desk, will almost certainly be disappointing. If you do have to film a gig, then try to get as much light on the stage as possible and avoid using any of the rig's red lights, if you can, as skin tones look bad in red-lit shots. Also avoid wearing highly patterned clothing, as this may make the shots strobe, and avoid clothing with commercial logos on it, as this might theoretically prevent the footage from being shown. If you're filming on more than one camera, go for a mixture of fixed 'safety' shots and moving hand-held footage, not forgetting (as many do) that if you have a drummer you should remember to get some shots of him or her from some sensible pre-selected vantage point.

Most great videos depend on one or two central ideas that make the video memorable and bear repeated viewing, and this doesn't necessarily involve having a large budget. The wide variety of editing software now available brings effects and editing techniques that only a few years ago would have cost thousands of pounds per day to create within the grasp of any reasonably competent and creative computer operator.

Alternatively, approach the students on any local film courses that might be running nearby. You might find one with access to a DV camera and editing software who is interested in putting together a promo clip for you.

It's unwise to attempt to produce a video yourselves, unless you have a clear creative vision of what you want to achieve and specialist knowledge. Unless the end product has been edited and dubbed at a professional editing suite to precise technical standards, it is unlikely to be technically suitable for broadcast, even if you managed to persuade a TV company to take an interest. This is no reflection on the technology at your disposal; it's simply a fact that television broadcasters have extremely high technical criteria to meet.

Having a video may be an interesting bonus in your attempts to get labels and managers interested, but it should take low priority when set against more basic groundwork like building up a local following.

# Licensing

Although the subject of licensing has been mentioned elsewhere in this book, the subject may have new relevance when a band actually has product commercially released and distributed in the UK. Firstly, most distribution deals will make product available outside the UK via export sales (where a foreign distributor decides to buy a quantity of your release to sell in their home territory) or via sales to overseas customers through online retailers.

Secondly, overseas labels and distributors might take a direct interest in a UK band with a commercial release – however low-key this is – if they feel that the band may be suitable for (for example) inclusion on a compilation album that they're releasing. Additionally, overseas journalists and DJs might also begin to take an interest in the band (although beware of emails from supposed DJs at obscure foreign radio stations trying to get free copies of your single to expand their own record collection). The fact remains that, since the advent of the Internet, the worldwide record market has never been easier to access. It is incredibly exciting for any new artists to discover that, for example, a club DJ in Tokyo has been playing your track, or that a journalist in San Francisco loves your band and is writing a great review of your record.

It is therefore perfectly possible that licensing enquiries will begin to come in, either directly to the band or to the 'label', or via the distributor. Initially, these are likely to relate to the inclusion of a particular track on a compilation album and won't be particularly financially attractive. However, as a basic rule of thumb, if the offer is made on a favoured-nations basis (ie if you are getting the best deal everyone else is getting) and the license is non-exclusive (ie you can do whatever else you like with that particular track), then it's worthy of serious consideration.

At the risk of repeating an earlier point, there are numerous UK artists who have carved out a great career for themselves overseas whilst making little impact at home – and it's a lot more fun headlining at a packed club in Madrid than playing first-on at the Dublin Castle to ten people...

# 'I Can't Find It In The Shops'

It might comfort you to know that even bands with major record deals get phone calls from their mums along the lines of, 'I'm in Woolworths and they say they've never heard of it.' This kind of comment is extremely irritating but not based in reality. Clearly, when dealing with a small manufacturing run, it's unlikely that CDs will magically appear in record racks all over the country. However, some shops will have stocked the release and may have sold out. If they have, then they may have decided not to re-order any more stock for their own reasons, or, they may be waiting for new stock. Alternatively, the record may not, in fact, be out yet. If you have proper distribution, it's vital that you clarify whether the 'label' (ie you) or the distributor is responsible for getting the release listed in Music Week, as most retailers rely on that publication's weekly list of new releases (as well as their own computer systems) as definitive evidence that a particular product has been released.

Thankfully, with the advent of online retailing and more efficient systems between shops and distributors, it should be possible for people who really want a particular record to find it.

# Conclusion

Making and releasing your own record, although essentially a straightforward business, involves a great deal of hard work, a lot of organisation and a certain amount of financial risk. On the other hand, it can be incredibly rewarding, creatively, and can provide real focus for any artist. If one were to take 50 UK acts that have gone on to achieve great success, particularly guitar bands, one would find that most of them began their career with some kind of independent release that gave an enormous boost to their prospects.

All bands in the early stages of their careers need to feel that things are on an upward curve. It's certainly far more satisfying, when somebody asks 'What's happening with the band?' to say, 'We've got our first single coming out in two months' than to say, 'Just doing a few gigs.'

# CHAPTER 9

# LAWYERS AND ACCOUNTANTS

No artist has been able to sustain a successful career path without the advice and guidance of specialist lawyers and accountants, whose role is to take care of the legal, contractual and financial aspects of his or her career. Once an artist's career has developed to the extent that contracts need signing and money is coming in, the advice of professionals is vital.

All too often, artists who are on the verge of becoming successful are at the mercy of an incredibly busy schedule and often can't even organise paying domestic bills, let alone keep an eye on the finances of their 'business'. It's also fair to say that many creative people find legal and financial issues mind-numbingly boring and often assume that things are being taken care of when they are not. It's very depressing to read stories about seemingly successful artists who have ended up with very little money, either by being ripped off or by making bad decisions. In these cases, there has usually been a deadly combination of poor professional advice and lack of interest from the artist.

# Lawyers

By 'lawyers', most people mean solicitors. There are many firms of solicitors – mostly based in London – that have departments solely dedicated to work in the entertainment industry. Although the situation in the UK hasn't yet reached the stage it has in the USA, where artists seem to have lawyers almost before they've bought their first instrument, there's no doubt that the role of music-industry solicitors is becoming more and more high-profile, at an ever earlier stage in artists' careers.

It is important to differentiate between actual solicitors and more general firms that offer advice on the legal and business-affairs aspects of the music industry. One important difference is that solicitors must hold what's known as 'professional indemnity insurance', which means that their clients have some hope of compensation if they suffer losses as a result of the solicitor's advice, perhaps after having sued the solicitor.

There are, however, companies that offer legal and business affairs advice to artists and which usually have personnel with a background working in the Business Affairs departments of record labels and publishers.

In the main, music-business solicitors are less involved in offering straight advice on points of law than in dealing with the commercial negotiations and contractual disputes that are part and parcel of the industry. Solicitors thus become keenly aware of all the latest bargaining positions taken by record companies, publishers and managers, as they are dealing with them on a daily basis.

At the risk of repeating myself, it is extremely dangerous to instruct a solicitor who doesn't regularly deal with music industry matters. This is not only because he or she may not be aware that a particular issue is crucially important to a negotiation, due to his unfamiliarity with the terminology of the business, but also because he is unlikely to have any idea whether the money and royalty rates under discussion are in keeping with current deals on offer in the industry.

# Finding A Solicitor

You'll need the advice of a solicitor almost as soon as you're offered any kind of a deal, be it management, recording or publishing. I've included a list of the better known solicitors in Appendix 4. The Musicians' Union also offers a basic legal service to its members.

Many firms offer a free initial consultation and also Legal Aid work, although it's fair to say that enquiries from new and inexperienced artists are often dealt with by the more junior members of a particular firm.

Most solicitors in London charge between £150 and £300 per hour for their advice, although some may agree a fixed price for negotiating a particular agreement. Almost all will ask for some money on account before commencing work, and you should be completely straight with them if there is a level beyond which you cannot afford to spend.

It may be intimidating to meet a solicitor for the first time, but remember that you are the client. You shouldn't be afraid to ask even the most basic questions if certain points are unclear. Most music business solicitors are fairly relaxed and informal, far removed from the stuffy and pompous image sometimes portrayed by their counterparts in some of the more boring areas of the law.

Most music business solicitors are very into music itself, and are used to dealing with artists and managers. Don't feel that you have to wear a suit and tie to get into their office! Many will make a habit of networking at gigs, and your lawyer may become a familiar sight at your London shows. Many solicitors will have an in-depth knowledge of the A&R community and may suggest that your demo – if it is attracting some interest – should also be sent to other labels, publishers and managers that you might not be aware of.

It's also true that certain solicitors do fancy themselves as A&R people and do cross the boundaries of their role in the scheme of things, to the extent that, on certain nights, London venue the Barfly can be uncomfortably packed with suits. The reality is that A&R people humour any such pretensions in order to keep solicitors on side, but the brutal truth is that you shouldn't get too excited if your solicitor thinks your material is great. Get excited when they negotiate you an amazing deal!

Solicitors also tend to be fairly blunt in their views of certain labels, publishers and managers. At the end of the day, your solicitor can't make you take his advice, but if he warns you of the dangers of signing to a particular company or individual, you should consider his advice carefully. If, for example, the solicitor has another client signed to a particular company and finds that company a nightmare to deal with, or knows that they're having financial problems, that is vital information.

# Your Solicitor In Negotiation

You should be immediately wary if your potential manager seems not to like your choice of solicitor. It's likely that this is because he has a reputation as a tough negotiator; rather, it may be because he knows that the solicitor is aware of aspects of his own reputation that you are not. Stick to your guns and don't be put off if your manager implies that he might decide not to sign you if your solicitor keeps being 'difficult'. If he really wants to manage you, he will. This can lead to a fairly tense atmosphere, however, so it's important to let your manager know that you're not just taking everything your solicitor says at face value and that you'll listen to his views with an open mind. After all, every point that your solicitor raises on the management agreement is likely to lose the manager money in real terms – the percentages will be knocked down, the Term reduced, and so on.

If you already have a manager, you shouldn't have used his solicitor to act for you when you negotiated the management agreement with him, as this would have been a conflict of interest. However, once the management deal is signed, you may decide to use the manager's solicitor to act for you in negotiating the publishing or record deal. The key point here is that the solicitor will need to know precisely whom he is taking his instructions from – the artists, or the manager on behalf of the artists. In practice, the manager usually communicates with the solicitor on behalf of the artists.

This can be dangerous in certain circumstances, however. It's very important for the artist not to leave the negotiation of a record deal to the manager and solicitor alone. The artist needs to understand which points have been given away and which are being stuck to. Most importantly, the artist needs to be aware which points are so-called 'deal breakers' – those which, unless they are agreed, will mean that the deal is off.

It's important to note that solicitors act upon 'instructions' from clients and don't unilaterally decide which way to respond when negotiating points. They will offer advice as to whether every point should be accepted or disputed, following which they will act on their client's instructions. For this reason, you need to be sure that a deal is proceeding without delays that may be caused by your solicitor waiting for your, or your manager's, instructions on a certain point. It is certainly the case that the best industry solicitors are extremely overworked, and it's easy for a potential deal to drift for a few days unless you keep the pressure up.

In most record and publishing deals, your solicitor will be negotiating either with the record label or with the publisher's in-house Business Affairs staff, or with another firm of solicitors retained to act for the label or publisher.

If deals hit problems, it's all too tempting for the label or publisher to contact the artist or manager direct and imply that their solicitor is causing difficulty on a particular point and that the deal may fall through as a result. This kind of brinkmanship is commonplace, and the artist or manager must be careful not to weaken their solicitor's bargaining position as a result of such pressures. If the solicitor is familiar with the deals being offered by certain labels and publishers, he will know just how far he can push a particular point.

At the end of the day, you're not going to get everything you want, whether from a label, a publisher or a manager. Labels, in particular, would rather lose a deal than cave in on certain points if doing so will cause them problems on their agreements with other artists. Remember, also, that your solicitor will be negotiating many deals with that particular company over the course of his career, and he will know when 'no' means 'no'.

The best deals, in reality, are those signed where both parties feel that they have the best possible terms and have left the negotiating table with their honour intact.

# Legal Costs

It's worth mentioning here that many record labels, publishers, and even some managers, will offer to pay for an artist's legal costs. A ceiling is almost always set, however, and any such payments are likely to be made recoupable, or rechargeable as an artist expense by a manager. It's very hard to offer examples of the levels of such costs; a recent legal bill for the very hard-fought negotiation of a major record and publishing deal for one particular artist was billed at a quite staggering £25,000. Perhaps between £3,000 and £5,000 for a major record deal or publishing deal, and £2,000 or so for a management deal, would be in the ballpark.

Be aware that some managers may use the offer of paying your legal fees as a way of influencing your choice of solicitor, and also that some such offers of payment are made conditional upon the deal being eventually signed. In other words, if you're unable to agree the deal, you may be left with a hefty legal bill.

It's best to be aware at all times that, if you talk to your solicitor or send them an email, it's going to cost you money. Guitar strings cost money. It's just one of the costs of being in business.

# Accountants

There are many accountancy firms that specialise in music industry work, and most are based in London. It's less easy to be specific about the right time for accountants to become involved in an artist's career. It's also true to say that many of the principles applied by accountants in their work don't uniquely apply to the music industry, unlike those of solicitors, and therefore that an 'everyday' accountant is less likely to damage an artist's career than a non-specialist solicitor.

It's likely that most new artists who have made some headway in gigging will have set up a simple bank or building society account to handle what income and costs they have, and this is perfectly adequate in the early stages. In the case of a band, it's probably best for whichever band member has the best credit record and relationship with their bank to open an account, for the time being. With the advent of online banking, it's easy for every member of the band to see where things stand at any one time.

You may have seen stories in the press in recent years concerning accountants who have 'borrowed' their clients' money, either to prop up their own businesses or to fund their own lifestyles or invest in business schemes. In these cases, the accountant has almost always been a signatory on a client account in which large sums have been deposited. There is no reason to suspect that this kind of activity is more prevalent in the music industry than anywhere else, but it's far too easy for busy artists who tour a lot to neglect their finances and not take enough of an interest in this supposedly boring area.

## Hiring An Accountant

If an artist is at the stage of having some money coming in and some expenses going out, having a basic set of books and setting up tax and National Insurance plans is vital.

It might also the case that some members of a newly signed band have had jobs, whereas some might have been on benefits, and so setting up the financial structure of the band from the outset is a job for an expert. Whatever the band's background, all of its members should try to attend the initial meetings at which the accountant is hired, and should try to take an equal interest in the finances of the band. Whether or not the manager is taking care of most of the day-today financial work, the fact is that money is the one issue that most bands are likely to fall out over, and is also a regular area of dispute with managers.

Probably the first question that will require an accountant's view is *how* you wish to trade. You can trade as a sole trader (or partnership, in the case of a band) or through a limited company, and each has its advantages and disadvantages.

Sole traders and partnerships are simpler trading entities than companies, but they involve personal liability if things go wrong – for example, if you cancelled a tour and an aggrieved promoter wanted to sue for his losses, he would sue the artist or band personally. Sole traders and partnerships are, however, generally cheaper to run, in terms of accountant's charges, as they require simpler accounts to be prepared.

If it's recommended that you trade as a partnership, you should ask tough questions about the possible dangers of personal liability. To spell out in blunt terms what 'liability' means, perhaps imagine the unappealing prospect of a large gentleman (commonly known as a 'bailiff') arriving unexpectedly at your rehearsal rooms, brandishing legal paperwork and seizing your instruments as payment for an unpaid debt.

You will also almost certainly be recommended to draw up a partnership agreement between the members of the band which will cover not just the financial side of things and the partners' obligations but also what will happen if things go wrong and one of the band wants to quit – who, for example, owns the band name? Your solicitor will be able to draft this type of agreement for you.

Using a company to provide your services to record labels, publishers and promoters (managers are unlikely to agree anything other than a contract for personal management) limits your liability when things go wrong, but it creates a more complex structure and is more expensive to administer – for example, because of the necessity of preparing audited accounts. It is likely that the members of a band would become equal shareholders and also directors of their service company, and income drawn from the company by the directors would be subject to PAYE.

One point worth repeating here is that record companies and publishers will almost certainly require the artist to sign an 'inducement letter' when they sign a deal with the artist's company. This means that, if at any point the company ceases to exist or loses the right to provide the artist's services, the artist is still personally signed to that deal.

# Business Managers

The concept of the business manager is primarily an American one, and such firms or individuals operate largely on the financial side of an artist's career, but get involved in the commercial aspects of deals and therefore, by default, some of the legalities. Some UK lawyers and accountants are now starting to style themselves as business managers and adopting the US approach of charging not only fees but a percentage of the artist's gross income.

The cynical view might be that the reason why business managers have found favour in the US is that some American artist managers have not, historically, been as adept at the business side of an artist's career as they might have been, and have preferred instead to delegate this role and give away a percentage. Whatever the reason, the UK music business and its artists are probably better served by the distinct roles of managers, lawyers and accountants, and by the simpler fee structures charged by professionals based on the actual work they do rather than on the value of the deals they are involved in negotiating.

# Budgeting

Whatever stage an artist is at, putting detailed budgeting in place is vital in order to be able to concentrate on the creative aspects of their career. Most signed artists, it's fair to say, pay themselves a fixed wage which may then increase during touring periods, for example. This is often augmented with bonuses after a particularly successful tour or on receipt of a large contractual advance or royalty payment.

It's very important to understand your cashflow as a signed band or published writer, particularly as the timing of the payment of advances may vary, depending on when product is delivered or when options are picked up. No artist wants to be in the position of returning from a three-month tour only to be told that next month's wages cheques can't be covered because an obvious gap in the cashflow has not been foreseen by the manager or the accountant.

# VAT

VAT may become an issue early on in your career. It is a sales tax levied on the sale of many goods and services in the UK by those individuals or companies whose turnover exceeds a certain level or who wish to be VAT registered, whatever their turnover. If you are registered for VAT, every three months you will be able to claim back the VAT that others charge you. You will, however, have to pay to HM Customs & Excise the VAT you've charged to others if it exceeds what you're claiming.

The current rate of VAT is 17.5%, so, if a studio charged you £1,000 for a session but you didn't spot in the small print on the booking form that you were also going to be charged VAT, the total bill will be £1,175. If you were registered for VAT, you could claim back the £175 you'd been charged. Every three months, you would fill in and sign a VAT return, which would detail the VAT you'd charged to people and the VAT that other people had charged you. If you'd paid out more than you'd charged, you would get a cheque for the difference. Similarly, if you're registered for VAT and charge somebody £100 to play a gig, you would have to add £17.50 of VAT on top.

You should also be aware that, if you're being paid for a gig on ticket sales, this will almost certainly mean that sales are net of VAT, if the promoter is VAT-registered. Thus, if a gig ticket was £10, including VAT, the net value of that ticket would go down to £8.50.

Registering for VAT is free and is compulsory if your turnover exceeds (currently) £52,500 per year. However, you will almost certainly have to pay an accountant to calculate your VAT and fill in your VAT return every three months, although it is possible to do the lion's share of the work yourself using a simple spreadsheet application to list all VAT receipts and invoices.

# CHAPTER 10

# MUSIC INDUSTRY ORGANISATIONS

There are numerous industry bodies that regulate or represent different areas of the music industry. At the initial stages of an artist's career, some of these organisations will have little relevance, but it is as well to understand their function. At the very least, membership of organisations such as those listed below by companies and individuals you may end up dealing with suggests that they are perhaps more serious contenders for your interest than those who are not.

The websites of the organisations listed below should be required viewing for anyone seeking an in-depth understanding of the music industry, particularly as many of them deal with income streams due to performers and writers. They will also provide links to other industry organisations that might be relevant to your career.

## The Musicians' Union

The MU is a trades union that represents and protects the interests of musicians. It negotiates with the record companies and their trade body, the BPI (see later), to conclude blanket agreements relating to (for example) payments to musicians for recording sessions and appearances in promo clips. It also negotiates with television and radio broadcasters on behalf of musicians, setting rates of payment for television and radio performances and repeat fees.

In addition, the MU offers legal advice to artists who are MU members, and favourable deals for equipment insurance. It publishes guidelines on session rates in the event that you're asked to perform as a session musician on a track by another artist, or perhaps to appear on a TV or radio show, and rates for live appearances.

The MU also chases up money owed to its members and offers legal and business affairs advice on contracts and disputes. It publishes the monthly members' magazine *Musician* and also directories of members, as well as informative leaflets on a wide variety of issues that affect musicians, such as recording contracts, gigging and managers.

There's no doubt that the MU has performed a vital function over the years in ensuring that its members are protected against the sometimes cut-throat aspects of the music business. It has been dogged in its dealings with the BPI and broadcasters, and has campaigned vigorously against issues in the live-music arena, such as 'pay to play', sometimes at the expense of its own image (it is still perceived by cynical observers as the haunt of old cabaret musos who last played second trombone in The Geoff Love Orchestra). Critics say that the MU isn't flexible enough to meet the commercial demands of the industry today – particularly in terms of the time it takes to obtain MU clearance for usage of old TV footage – and is obstructive and unhelpful in many areas. However, many broadcasters even today won't risk incurring the wrath of the MU on matters such as clearances, despite the demise of the closed shop, and many session fixers will still book only MU members.

On balance, I would say that all new artists should join the Musicians' Union. It is relatively inexpensive to join (currently £99 per year if you earn less than £15,000 per year from music), and subscription fees should be more than covered by savings on services that the MU can provide. It's important to maintain regular contact with the MU (it has a number of regional offices), keep paying the subs and notify them of any change of address. Their website is a mine of useful information.

Tel: 0207 582 5566
60–62 Clapham Road, London SW9 0JJ
Fax: 0207 582 9805
www.musiciansunion.org.uk

# MCPS (Mechanical-Copyright Protection Society)

Established in 1924, the MCPS was formed in order to administer the rights of music publishers. It represents its members – publishers and songwriters – in relation to the copying and reproduction of copies of works, in most cases by way of sound recordings. In doing so, it negotiates and concludes agreements with those who wish to use recordings on formats such as CD, cassette, vinyl and DVD. It sets rates for such usages, collects sums due for the·users and distributes these sums to its members. Currently, over 16,000 publishers and writers are members of the MCPS, and the Society distributed funds in excess of £220 million to its members in 2003.

Royalties are paid to the MCPS by a wide variety of users of music, with record and video companies, record and video manufacturers, record distributors, computer-game manufacturers and background music operators being the principal sources of its income. The MCPS funds its operations by charging its members commission, which is deducted from royalties generated – about 7% on average.

The relevance of the MCPS to a new artist could be that, when you've pressed a CD to send to record companies and sell at gigs, for example, you'll have to pay to the MCPS the mechanical royalties referred to earlier in Chapter 3. If you are the writer, and the CD is a limited run and not for sale, you should in theory be able to get away with not paying mechanical royalties. However, if the CD includes covers of other writers' songs, you will certainly have to pay 'mechanicals' on the CDs you sell. It's almost certain that the CD pressing plant will ask you to fill in a standard MCPS licence form before the CDs are pressed, as otherwise they may face punitive action from the Society.

In addition, it may be that a new band or group of solo writers decide to become writer or publisher members of the MCPS. This would be relevant if, for example, you had written a song that was to be covered by an artist who would be issuing CDs of the song – perhaps a signed artist. The MCPS would collect monies owed to you, as the writer or publisher, and distribute them to you.

Tel: 0207 580 5544
29–33 Berners Street, London W1T 3AB
Fax: 0207 306 4455
www.mcps.co.uk

# PRS (Performing Rights Society)

The PRS acts on behalf of its members, who are songwriters and music publishers, in order to license the public performance, broadcast and cable transmission of works and then collect and distribute any monies due. You've probably seen PRS stickers in cafes and pubs that use either live or piped music, the reason being that such usage of music requires the venue in question to pay an annual fee to the PRS.

The PRS was formed in 1914 and currently has in excess of 40,000 writer and publisher members. It distributes annual income of over £250 million.

Royalties are paid to the PRS by users of music for public performance, including TV and radio broadcasters, cable operators, venues, clubs, airlines, hotels, restaurants and so on. Like the MCPS, it funds its operations by levying an administration fee before distributing its royalties. In 1993, the MCPS and the PRS entered into an alliance on a practical level which enabled works to be registered with the MCPS and their details registered simultaneously with the PRS. Since then, the two organisations have combined many of their data-storage and clearance functions, establishing joint teams in areas such as Finance and Business Affairs, with the aim of reducing costs and thus, in theory, commissions charged to members.

The relevance of joining the PRS is the same as for joining the MCPS: if you are the writer or publisher of works that are to be performed in public, the PRS will collect and distribute monies owed to you. For example, it's not too far-fetched to imagine that you might get a support tour with a major act playing large halls, in which case filling in the details of your set list on a PRS form after every show will lead to a small but significant slice of income once the distribution is made. In order to join the Society, you'll need to have works that are already being performed and commercially available (ie released on record).

The main equivalent organisations in the USA are ASCAP (American Society of Composers, Authors and Publishers) and the BMI (Broadcast Music Incorporated), both of which license the broadcast and public performance of music controlled by their members (ASCAP) or affiliates (BMI) who are songwriters and publishers. The difference between the two is essentially that ASCAP is owned by its members and the BMI is a corporation controlled by radio and television broadcasters. If you're the writer or publisher of works that are likely to be performed in the USA, you'll need to join one of these organisations in order to ensure that income due is distributed to you.

Tel: 0207 580 5544
29–33 Berners Street, London W1T 3AB
Fax: 0207 306 4455
www.prs.co.uk

# BPI (British Phonographic Industry)

The BPI is a trade association that represents more than 200 UK record companies, including all of the majors and most of the better-known independents. Its aim is to protect and advance the interests of the UK record industry, and as such the BPI is effectively responsible for the profile of the UK industry at Government and international trade level. The BPI organises the annual BRIT Awards, which are becoming one of the most significant televised music events in the world, and contributes to events such as National Music Day. It is also responsible for certifying and issuing silver, gold and platinum discs based on UK sales of albums and singles. The BPI also involves itself in events such as the Sound City Festivals each year and has set up the BRIT School for Performing Arts and Technology, near Croydon, in partnership with the Department of Trade and Industry.

Outside such high-profile activities, the BPI lobbies the Government and the members of the EU on matters affecting the industry and the music business in general. It campaigns against piracy, co-ordinating international action in league with the IFPI (International Federation of the Phonographic Industry). It negotiates with bodies such as the Musicians' Union on issues such as session rates and repeat fees, and with the MCPS on all issues affecting its members' rights to use copyrights controlled by MCPS members.

On the international stage, the BPI has the effective responsibility of presenting the image of British music abroad, through participation in trade events such as MIDEM, in Cannes, every year and PopKomm, in Germany, where BPI members benefit from a strong UK industry profile in their efforts to export music abroad. The BRIT Awards TV show assists enormously with these efforts by being syndicated to most countries.

Tel: 0207 803 1300
Riverside Building, County Hall, Westminster Bridge Road, London SE1 7JA
Fax: 0207 803 1310
www.bpi.co.uk

# Agents' Association (Great Britain)

The Agents' Association represents a large number of entertainment agents (ie booking agents), and you might find yourself dealing with an agent early on in your live career. Usually, such an agent will have the Association's logo prominently displayed on their stationery and contracts, many of which contracts are in standard form. The Association's members have agreed to abide by its code of professional ethics and other codes of conduct, and in turn the Association can be said to represent the vast majority of reputable agents in the UK. If, for example, you had a dispute with an agent over non-payment of a fee, you could refer the matter to the Association for arbitration or make a complaint direct to the Association.

Tel: 0207 834 0515
54 Keyes House, Dolphin Square, London SW1V 3NA
Fax: 0207 821 0261
www.agents-uk.com

# PPL (Phonographic Performance Limited) And VPL (Video Performance Limited)

PPL licenses the broadcasting and public performance of sound recordings and thus negotiates agreements with organisations such as television and radio stations, charging fees to such users. The fees collected are then distributed to members, which include record companies and also the performers who appeared on the recordings, in a similar way to PAMRA (see later).

All music videos produced by VPL members (who are mainly record companies) are assigned a unique code number, which is logged by broadcasters every time the video is shown. The broadcasters then pay a fee to VPL according to whatever blanket agreement they have negotiated with the organisation. If you've made a broadcast-quality promo clip and wish to submit it to broadcasters, it's as well to join VPL and ensure that the identification code for your clip is set out on the front 'clock' of the video.

Tel: 0207 534 1000
1 Upper James Street, London W1F 9DE
Fax: 0207 534 1111
www.ppluk.com

# MPA (Music Publishers' Association)

The MPA performs a similar function for music publishers as the BPI does for record labels, providing a forum for advancing and protecting the business of music publishing. It owns MCPS as its subsidiary and is a non-profit-making organisation.

The MPA campaigns on all issues relating to copyright protection and is also involved heavily in the gradual merging of the activities of the PRS and the MCPS. The MPA does not, however, have any role in the licensing of the reproduction or performance of its members' work.

As with the BPI, the fact that a publishing company that's expressing an interest in you is a member of the MPA indicates that they are more likely to be a 'proper' publisher than a company or individual who is not a member.

Tel: 0207 839 7779
3rd Floor, Strandgate, 18–20 York Buildings, London WC2N 6JU
Fax: 0207 839 7776
www.mpaonline.org.uk

# IMMF (International Music Managers' Forum)

The IMMF is a forum run by artist managers and was set up in 1992 by a coalition of powerful artist managers led by the team managing Simply Red. Whilst by no means all artist managers are members of the IMMF, and record companies and publishers have been somewhat reserved about giving credence to it, there is no doubt that the IMMF is a relevant organisation. The principal reason for this is that the interests of managers usually mirror those of their clients, the artists, in lobbying against some of the less artist-friendly aspects of the industry.

Another important function of the IMMF has been to recognise that there has been almost no formal education and training for new managers entering the industry and, accordingly, to support seminars and other educational events devoted to management training. As mentioned earlier in this book, artist managers are not renowned for their altruism and team spirit, and it's dog-eat-dog in the competition for new clients. However, any co-operation between managers in dealing with the might of organisations such as the BPI has to be welcomed. On a personal level, I wouldn't make any judgment about the merits of a manager on the basis of whether or not they were in the IMMF; after all, Groucho Marx once said that he didn't want to join any club that would have him as a member, and the same thing applies here!

It's important to note that the IMMF does not provide artists with help in finding a manager.

Tel: 0207 935 2446
1 York Street, London W1U 6PA
Fax: 0207 486 6045
www.immf.net

# AIM (Association Of Independent Music)

AIM is a trade body representing around 500 UK independent labels, including such significant names as V2, Mute and One Little Indian. It campaigns on behalf of the interests of its members and promotes British independent music. It also provides a negotiating body for agreements without outside parties concerning issues affecting its members.

AIM also offers business advice and training for new independent labels, as well as inroads into foreign markets.

Tel: 0208 994 5599
Lamb House, Church Street, London W4 2PD
Fax: 0208 994 5222
www.musicindie.org

# PAMRA (Performing Artists' Media Rights Association)

PAMRA distributes money to performers who have played on recordings that have been released commercially and have been played in public. Performers' rights to receive a share of this money have existed only since 1996. This money arises through payments from broadcasters to PPL (see above), which distributes a proportion to the record labels that are its members and another proportion to performers via PAMRA.

It is free to join PAMRA; the organisation levies a small percentage of the income it collects to fund its operations.

Tel: 0207 940 0400
161 Borough High Street, London SE1 1HR
Fax: 0207 407 2008
www.pamra.org.uk

# EPILOGUE

Hopefully, after wading through this book, you'll be in better shape to go out there and get a deal. Think carefully about your commitment to your music and, if you're in a band, think about how committed the other band members are.

Could you spend months, or even years, touring up and down the motorways of the UK in a Transit for ten hours a day, living on Ginsters' pasties?

Could they?

Do you all get on, or do you secretly hate each other?

Are you prepared for constant rejection, with only your belief in your music to see you through?

Can you live on next to nothing rather than keep your job?

Are you willing to gamble everything if a deal comes your way? If you're not, there are plenty of musicians who are.

Good luck!

# APPENDIX 1

## Record Companies

An exhaustive list of the UK's record labels would take an entire book in itself, but the companies listed below are some of the major players and also the smaller labels with some interesting artists signed to them. As A&R people and talent scouts change companies on a fairly regular basis, it would be difficult to list individual names with any degree of long term accuracy. However, a visit to the websites listed below should show a company's current roster.

### 4AD
Tel: 0208 870 9724 • Fax: 0208 874 6600
17-19 Alma Road, London SW18 1AA
www.4ad.com

### 14th Floor Recordings
Tel: 0207 368 2500 • Fax: 0207 368 2788
The Warner Building, 28A Kensington Church St, London W8 4EP

### 679 Records
Tel: 0207 284 5780 • Fax: 0207 284 5795
172A Arlington Road, London NW1 7HL
www.679recordings.com

### Adventure Records
Tel: 0208 762 0101 • Fax: 0208 749 3600
Units 4c/4d Westpoint, 36/37 Warple Way, London W3 0RG
www.adventure-records.com

### All Around The World
Tel: 01254 264120 • Fax: 01254 693768
9-13 Penny Street, Blackburn, Lancashire BB1 6HJ
www.aatw.com

### Atlantic Records
Tel: 0207 938 5500 • Fax: 0207 368 4900
Electric Lighting Station, 46 Kensington Court, London W8 5DA
www.atlanticrecords.co.uk

### B-Unique Records
Tel: 0207 384 6460 • Fax: 0207 384 6466
Studios 30-32, The Matrix Studio Complex, 91 Peterborough Road, London SW6 3BU
www.b-uniquerecords.com

### Beggars Banquet
Tel: 0208 870 9912 • Fax: 0208 871 1766
17-19 Alma Road, London SW18 1AA
www.xl-recordings.com

179

## Big Cat Records
Tel: 0207 471 3280 • Fax: 0207 471 3288
PO Box 34449, London W6 0RT

## Blanco Y Negro
Tel: 0208 960 9888 • Fax: 0208 968 6715
66 Goldborne Road, London W10 5PS
www.roughtraderecords.com

## BMG / RCA
Tel: 0207 384 7500 • Fax: 0207 371 9298
Bedford House, 69-79 Fulham High Street, London SW6 3JW
www.click2music.co.uk

## Century Media Records
Tel: 0207 482 0161 • Fax: 0207 482 3165
6 Water Lane, Camden, London NW1 8NZ
www.centurymedia.net

## Cooking Vinyl
Tel: 0208 600 9200 • Fax: 0208 743 7448
10 Allied Way, London W3 0RQ
www.cookingvinyl.com

## Db Records
Tel: 01255 782 322
PO Box 19318, Bath, Somerset BA1 6ZS
www.dbrecords.co.uk

## Decca Music Group
Tel: 0208 747 8787 • Fax: 0208 994 2834
347-353 Chiswick High Road, London W4 4HS
www.deccaclassics.com

## Defected Records Ltd
Tel: 0207 439 9995 • Fax: 0207 432 6470
14-15 D'Arblay Street, London W1F 8DY
www.defected.co.uk

## Deltasonic Records
Tel: 0151 724 4760 • Fax: 0151 724 6286
102 Rose Lane, Mossley Hill, Liverpool L18 8AG
www.deltamusic.co.uk

## Eagle Records
Tel: 0208 870 5670 • Fax: 0208 874 2333
Eagle House, 22 Armoury Way, London SW18 1EZ
www.eagle-rock.com

# Echo

Tel: 0207 229 1616 • Fax: 0207 465 6296
Chrysalis Building, 13 Bramley Road, London W10 6SP
www.echo.co.uk

# Edel UK Records Ltd

Tel: 0207 482 4848 • Fax: 0207 482 4846
12 Oval Road, London, NW1 7DH
www.edel.com

# EMI

Tel: 0207 605 5000 • Fax: 0207 605 5050
EMI House, 43 Brook Green, London W6 7EF
www.emimusic.co.uk

# Fantastic Plastic

Tel: 0207 263 2267 • Fax: 0207 263 2268
The Church, Archway Close, London N19 3TD
www.fantasticplastic.co.uk

# Fierce Panda

Tel: 0207 609 2789 • Fax: 0207 609 8034
39 Tollington Road, London N7 6PB
www.fiercepanda.co.uk

# Fire Records

Tel: 0208 806 9922 • Fax: 0208 806 8021
21a Maury Road, London N16 7BP
www.firerecords.com

# Gut Recordings

Tel: 0207 266 0777 • Fax: 0207 266 7734
Byron House, 112a Shirland Road, London W9 2EQ
www.gutrecords.com

# Heavenly Recordings

Tel: 0207 494 2998 • Fax: 0207 437 3317
47 Frith Street, London W1D 4SE
www.heavenly100.com

# Hut Recordings

Tel: 0208 964 6107 • Fax: 0208 964 6196
Kensal House, 553-579 Harrow Road, London W10 4RH
www.hutrecordings.com

# Illustrious

Tel: 0207 911 8270 • Fax: 0207 911 8287
10 Great Marlborough Street, London W1F 7LP
www.illustriousrecords.com

## Independiente
Tel: 0208 747 8111 • Fax: 0208 747 8113
The Drill Hall, 3 Heathfield Terrace, London W4 4JE
www.independiente.co.uk

## Innocent
Tel: 0208 962 5800 • Fax: 0208 962 5801
Kensal House, 553-579 Harrow Road, London W10 4RH
www.virginrecords.co.uk

## Instant Karma
Tel: 0207 851 0900 • Fax: 0207 851 0901
36 Sackville Street, London W1S 3EQ
www.instantkarma.co.uk

## Island Records
Tel: 0208 910 3333 • Fax: 0208 748 1998
22 St Peters Square, London W6 9NW
www.umusic.com

## Jive Records
Tel: 0208 459 8899 • Fax: 0208 451 3900
Zomba House, 165-167 High Road, London NW10 2SG

## Matador Records Ltd
Tel: 0208 969 5533 • Fax: 0208 969 6633
PO Box 20125
www.matadoreurope.com

## Mercury Records
Tel: 0207 705 4200 • Fax: 0207 705 4201
PO Box 1425, 136-140 New Kings Road, London SW6 4FX
www.mercuryrecords.com

## Ministry Of Sound Recordings
Tel: 0207 378 6528 • Fax: 0207 403 5348
103 Gaunt Street, London SE1 6DP
www.ministryofsound.com

## Mute Records Ltd
Tel: 0208 964 2001 • Fax: 0208 968 4977
429 Harrow Road, London W10 4RE
www.mute.com

## Nettwerk Productions UK
Tel: 0207 424 7500 • Fax: 0207 424 7501
Clearwater Yard, 35 Iverness Street, London NW1 7HB
www.nettwerk.com

## One Little Indian
Tel: 0207 772 7600 • Fax: 0207 772 7601
34 Trinity Crescent, London SW17 7AE
www.indian.co.uk

## Parlophone
Tel: 0207 605 5000 • Fax: 0207 605 5050
EMI House, 43 Brook Green, London W6 7EF
www.parlophone.co.uk

## Placid Casual
Tel: 02920 394 200 • Fax: 02920 372 703
104a Cowbridge Road East, Canton, Cardiff CF11 9DX

## Polydor Records
Tel: 0208 910 4800 • Fax: 0208 910 4801
72-80 Black Lion Lane, London W6 9BE
www.polydor.co.uk

## Reverb Records Ltd
Tel: 0208 747 0660 • Fax: 0208 747 0880
Reverb House, Bennett Street, London W4 2AH
www.reverbxl.com

## Roadrunner Records
Tel: 0208 749 2984 • Fax: 0208 749 2523
Suite A, Tech West House, Warple Way, London W3 0UE
www.roadrunnerrecords.co.uk

## Rough Trade
Tel: 0208 960 9888 • Fax: 0208 968 6715
66 Goldborne Road, London W10 5PS
www.roughtraderecords.com

## Sanctuary Records Group
Tel:0207 602 6351 • Fax: 0207 603 5941
Sanctuary House, 45-53 Sinclair Road, London W14 0NS
www.sanctuaryrecordsgroup.co.uk

## Setanta Records
Tel: 0207 284 4877 • Fax: 0207 284 4577
174 Camden Road, London NW1 9HJ
www.setantarecords.com

## Skint Records
Tel: 01273 738 527 • Fax: 01273 208 766
PO Box 174, Brighton, East Sussex BN1 4BA
www.skint.net

## Sony Music Entertainment
Tel: 0207 911 8200 • Fax: 0207 911 8600
10 Great Marlborough Street, London W1V 2LP
www.sonymusic.com

## Southern Fried Records
Tel: 0207 800 4488 • Fax: 0207 736 4237
Fulham Palace, Bishops Avenue, London SW6 6EA
www.southernfriedrecords.com

## Taste Media Ltd
Tel: 0208 780 3311 • Fax: 0208 785 9892
263 Putney Bridge Road, London SW15 2PU
www.tastemedia.com

## Too Pure
Tel: 0208 875 6208 • Fax: 0208 875 1205
17-19 Alma Road, London SW18 1AA
www.toopure.co.uk

## Universal Classics & Jazz (UCJ)
Tel: 0208 910 3113 • Fax: 0208 910 3151
22 St Peters Square, London W6 9NW
www.universalclassics.com

## Universal Music (UK)
Tel: 0208 910 5000
PO Box 1420, 1 Sussex Place, London W6 9XS
Fax: 0208 741 4901
www.umusic.com

## Virgin Records
Tel: 0208 964 6000 • Fax: 0208 968 6533
Kensal House, 553-579 Harrow Road, London W10 4RH
www.virginrecords.co.uk

## V2 Records
Tel: 0207 471 3000 • Fax: 0207 603 4796
131-133 Holland Park Avenue, London W11 4UT
www.v2music.com

## Warner Music (UK) Ltd
Tel: 0207 937 8844 • Fax: 0207 938 3901
The Warner Building, 28 Kensington Church Street, London W8 4EP
www.warnermusic.co.uk

## WEA Records
Tel: 0207 761 6000 • Fax: 0207 761 6062
Waldron House, 57-63 Old Church Street, London SW3 5BS
e-mail: firstname.lastname@warnermusic.com

## XL Recordings
Tel: 0208 870 7511 • Fax: 0208 871 4178
1 Codrington Mews, London W11 2EH
www.xl-recordings.com

## ZTT Records
Tel: 0207 221 5101 • Fax: 0207 221 3374
The Blue Building, 42-46 St Lukes Mews, London W11 1DG
www.ztt.com

# APPENDIX 2

## Music Publishers

The following companies are some of the more active and successful in the UK. As we have seen in the chapter on publishing, many smaller companies are having enormous success with particular artists and writers. However, it is likely that such smaller publishers are probably sub-published or administered by one of the companies below.

### 4AD Music
Tel: 0208 871 2121 • Fax: 0208 871 2745
17-19 Alma Road, London SW18 1AA

### 19 Music
Tel: 0207 801 1919 • Fax: 0207 801 1919
Unit 32, Ransomes Dock, 35-37 Parkgate Road, London SW11 4NP

### Big Life Music
Tel: 0207 323 3888 • Fax: 0207 636 3551
67-69 Chalton Street, London NW1 1HY
www.biglife.co.uk

### BMG Music Publishing Ltd
Tel: 0207 384 7600 • Fax: 0207 384 8164
Bedford House, 69-79 Fulham Road, London SW6 3JW
www.bmgmuscisearch.com

### Bright Music
Tel: 0207 751 9935 • Fax: 0207 731 9314
21c Heathmans Road, Parsons Green, London SW6 4TJ
www.brightmusic.co.uk

### Carlin Music Corporation
Tel: 0207 734 3251 • Fax: 0207 439 2391
Iron Bridge House, 3 Bridge Approach, London NW1 8BD
e-mail: enquiries@carlinmusic.com

### Chrysalis Music
Tel: 0207 221 2213 • Fax: 0207 465 6178
The Chrysalis Building,13 Bramley Road, London W10 6SP
www.chrysalis.com

### Complete Music Ltd
Tel: 0207 731 8595 • Fax: 0207 371 5665
3rd Floor, Bishops Park House, 25-29 Fulham High Street, London SW6 3JH
www.complete-music.co.uk

## Dharma Music
Tel: 0207 851 0900 • Fax: 0207 851 0901
36 Sackville Street, London W1S 3EQ

## EMI Music Publishing
Tel: 0207 434 2131 • Fax: 0207 434 3531
127 Charing Cross Road, London WC2H 0QY
www.emimusicpub.co.uk

## Fairwood Music
Tel: 0207 487 5044 • Fax: 0207 935 2270
72 Marleybone Lane, London W1U 2PL

## Famous Music Publishing
Tel: 0207 736 7543 • Fax: 0207 471 4812
Bedford House, 69-79 Fulham High Street, London SW6 3JW
www.syncsite.com

## Gut Music
Tel: 0207 266 0777 • Fax: 0207 266 7734
Byron House, 112a Shirland Road, London W9 2EQ
www.gutrecords.com

## Heavenly Songs
Tel: 0207 494 2998 • Fax: 0207 437 3317
47 Frith Street, London W1D 4SE
www.heavenly100.com

## Hornall Bros Music
Tel: 0208 877 3366 • Fax: 0208 874 3131
1 Northfields Prospect, Putney Bridge Road, London SW18 1PE
www.hobro.co.uk

## Independent Music Group (IMG) Ltd
Tel: 0208 523 9000 • Fax: 0208 523 8888
Independent House, 54 Larkshall Road, London E4 6PD
www.independentmusicgroup.com

## Kojam Music
Tel: 0207 434 5151 • Fax: 0207 434 5155
33 Glasshouse Street, London W1B 5DG
www.kojammusic.com

## MCS Music Ltd
Tel: 0207 255 8777 • Fax: 0207 255 8778
32 Lexington Street, London W1F 0LQ
www.mcsmusic.com

## Minder Music
Tel: 0207 289 7281 • Fax: 0207 289 2648
8 Pindock Mews, London W9 2PY
www.mindermusic.com

## Ministry Of Sound Music Publishing Ltd
Tel: 0207 378 6528 • Fax: 0207 403 5348
103 Gaunt Street, London SE1 6DP
www.ministryofsound.com

## Mute Song
Tel: 0208 964 2001 • Fax: 0208 968 4977
Lawford House, 429 Harrow Road, London W10 4RE
www.mute.com

## Notting Hill Music
Tel: 0207 243 2921 • Fax: 0207 243 2894
Bedford House, 8B Berkeley Gardens, London W8 4AP
e-mail: info@nottinghillmusic.com

## Peermusic (UK)
Tel: 0207 404 7200 • Fax: 0207 404 7004
Peer House, 8-14 Verulam Street, London WC1X 8LZ
www.peermusic.com

## Perfect Songs
Tel: 0207 221 5101 • Fax: 0207 221 3374
The Blue Building, 42-46 St Luke's Mews, London W11 1DG
e-mail: rob@spz.com

## Reverb Music Limited
Tel: 0208 747 0660 • Fax: 0208 747 0880
Reverb House, Bennett Street, London W4 2AH
www.reverbxl.com

## Sanctuary Music Publishing
Tel: 0207 300 1866 • Fax: 0207 300 1881
Sanctuary House, 45-53 Sinclair Road, London W14 0NS
www.sanctuarygroup.com

## Sony/ATV Music Publishing
Tel: 0207 911 8200 • Fax: 0207 911 8600
13 Great Marlborough Street, London W1V 2LP
e-mail: firstname_lastname@uk.sonymusic.com

## Universal Music Publishing Limited
Tel: 0208 752 2600 • Fax: 0208 752 2601
Elsinore House, 77 Fulham Palace Road, London W6 8JA
e-mail: firstname.lastname@umusic.com

## Untouchable Songs
Tel: 0207 012 1400 • Fax: 0207 012 1434
2nd Floor, 81 Rivington Street, London EC2A 3AY

## V2 Music Publishing Ltd
Tel: 0207 471 3000 • Fax: 0207 471 3110
131-133 Holland Park Avenue, London W11 4UT
www.v2music.com

## Warner/Chappell Music Ltd
Tel: 0207 938 0000 • Fax: 0207 368 2777
Griffin House, 161 Hammersmith Road, London W6 8BS
www.warnerchappell.com

## Westbury Music Ltd
Tel: 0207 733 5400 • Fax: 0207 733 4449
Suite B, 2 Tunstall Road, London SW9 8DA
www.westburymusic.net

## Windswept Music (London) Ltd
Tel: 0208 237 8400 • Fax: 0208 741 0825
Hope House, 40 St Peter's Road, London W6 9DB
www.windswept.co.uk

# APPENDIX 3

## Management Companies

The following management companies represent some of the biggest artists in the business, and also some of the more exciting new artists. I have not listed examples of each company's clients for two reasons. Firstly, artists change their managers on a reasonably regular basis and it would thus be difficult to give information that would remain accurate for long. Secondly, it would be unfair to pigeonhole companies as representing only certain types of artists by listing their current clients. There are, of course, numerous companies and individuals not listed below who may have excellent artist management skills and experience.

### Big Life Management
Tel: 0207 554 2100 • Fax: 0207 554 2154
67-69 Chalton Street, London NW1 1HY
www.biglife.co.uk

### Terry Blamey Management
Tel: 0207 371 7627 • Fax: 0207 731 7578
PO Box 13196, London SW6 4WF

### Blujay Management
Tel: 0207 604 3633 • Fax: 0207 604 3639
55 Loudoun Road, London NW8 0DL
www.blujay.co.uk

### Stephen Budd Management
Tel: 0207 916 3303 • Fax: 0207 916 3302
109b Regents Park Road, London NW1 8UR
www.record-producers.com

### CMO Management (International) Ltd
Tel: 0207 524 7700 • Fax: 0207 524 7701
Studio 223, Westbourne Studios, 242 Acklam Road, London W10 5JJ

### EG Management Ltd
Tel: 0208 540 9935
PO Box 4397, London W1A 7RZ

### First Column Management Ltd
Tel: 01273 688 359 • Fax: 01273 624 884
The Metway, 55 Canning Street, Brighton BN2 0EF

### Friars Management
Tel: 01296 434731 • Fax: 01296 422530
33 Alexander Road, Aylesbury, Bucks HP20 2NR
www.fmlmusic.com

## Gailforce Management
Tel: 0207 584 5977 • Fax: 0207 838 0351
30 Ives Street, London SW3 2ND

## GR Management
Tel: 0141 632 1111 • Fax: 0141 649 0042
974 Pollockshaws Road, Shawlands, Glasgow G41 2HA

## Ignition Music
Tel: 0207 298 6000 • Fax: 0207 258 0962
54 Linhope Street, London NW1 6HL

## JPR Management
Tel: 0208 749 8874 • Fax: 0208 749 8774
Unit 4 E & F, Westpoint, 33-34 Warple Way, London W3 0RG
www.jprmanagement.co.uk

## Massive Management
Tel: 01424 812 945 • Fax: 01424 812 420
The Seahouse, Pett Level Road, Pett Level, East Sussex TN35 4EH
www.qedtheband.com

## MCM
Tel: 0207 580 4088 • Fax: 0207 580 4098
Third Floor, 40 Langham Street, London W1N 5RG

## 19 Management
Tel: 0207 801 1919 • Fax: 0207 801 1920
33 Ransomes Dock, 35-37 Parkgate Road, London SW11 4NP
www.19.co.uk

## Out There Management
Tel: 0207 739 6903 • Fax: 0207 613 2715
Strongroom, 120-124 Curtain Road, London EC2A 3SQ

## Part Rock Management Ltd
Tel: 0207 224 1992 • Fax: 0207 224 0111
Level 2, 65 Newman Street, London W1T 3EG

## Principle Management
Tel: 00 353 1 677 7330 • Fax: 00 353 1 677 7276
30-32 Sir John Rogersons Quay, Dublin 2, Ireland

## Pure Management
Tel: 07747 152 524
18 Chilham Place, Macclesfield, Cheshire SK11 8TG
www.pureacts.com

## Riverman Management
Tel: 0207 381 4000 • Fax: 0207 381 9666
Top Floor, George House, Brecon Road, London W6 8PY
www.riverman.co.uk

## Safe Management
Tel: 01276 476 676 • Fax: 01276 451 109
St Ann's House, Guildford Road, Lightwater, Surrey GU18 5RA

## Sanctuary Artist Management
Tel: 0207 602 6351 • Fax: 0207 603 5941
Sanctuary House, 45-53 Sinclair Road, London W14 0NS
www.sanctuarygroup.com

## Schoolhouse Management
Tel: 0131 557 4242
42 York Place, Edinburgh EH1 3HU
www.schoolhousemanagement.co.uk

## Sincere Management
Tel: 0208 960 4438 • Fax: 0208 968 8458
Flat B, 6 Bravington Road, London W9 3AH

## Doug Smith Associates
Tel: 0208 993 8436 • Fax: 0208 896 1778
PO Box 1151, London W3 82J
www.dougsmithassociates.com

## Trinifold Management
Tel: 0207 419 4300 • Fax: 0207 419 4325
Third Floor, 12 Oval Road, London NW1 7DH

## Value Added Talent Management (VAT)
Tel: 0207 704 9720 • Fax: 0207 226 6135
1-2 Purley Place, London N1 1QA
www.vathq.co.uk

## Stephen Wells Management
Tel: 0207 372 5488 • Fax: 0207 372 5488
9 Woodchurch Road, London NW6 3PL

## Wildlife Entertainment
Tel: 0207 371 7008 • Fax: 0207 371 7708
Unit F, 21 Heathmans Road, London SW6 4TJ

## XL Talent Partnership
Tel: 0208 747 0660 • Fax: 0208 747 0880
Reverb House, Bennett Street, London W4 2AH
www.reverbxl.com

# APPENDIX 4

## Music Business Solicitors

The following firms specialise in music industry work. Whilst many other firms both in London and the regions have music business experience, you should be absolutely certain that the solicitor you instruct is a specialist in this area and is fully up to date with the current commercial negotiating positions taken in the industry. I have dealt with most of the following firms and would recommend them.

### Addleshaw Goddard
Tel: 0207 606 8855 • Fax: 0207 606 4390
150 Aldersgate Street, London EC1A 4EJ
www.addleshawgoddard.com

### SJ Berwin & Co
Tel: 0207 533 2222 • Fax: 0207 533 2000
222 Grays Inn Road, London WC1X 8HB
www.sjberwin.com

### Bray & Krais Solicitors
Tel: 0207 493 8840 • Fax: 0207 493 8841
42 Southwick Street, London W2 1JQ
www.brayandkrais.com

### Clintons
Tel: 0207 379 6080 • Fax: 0207 240 9310
55 Drury Lane, London WC2B 5RZ
www.clintons.co.uk

### Davenport Lyons
Tel: 0207 468 2600 • Fax: 0207 437 8216
1 Old Burlington Street, London W1X 2NL
www.davenportlyons.com

### David, Wineman
Tel: 0207 400 7800 • Fax: 0207 400 7890
Craven House, 121 Kingsway, London WC2B 6NX
www.davidwineman.co.uk

### P Ganz & Co
Tel: 0208 293 9103 • Fax: 0208 355 9560
88 Calvert Road, Greenwich, London SE10 0DF

### Goldkorn, Mathias, Gentle
Tel: 0207 631 1811 • Fax: 0207 631 0431
6 Coptic Street, London WC1A 1NW

## Harbottle & Lewis
Tel: 0207 667 5000 • Fax: 0207 667 5100
Hanover House, 14 Hanover Square, London W1S 1HP
www.harbottle.co.uk

## Lee & Thompson
Tel: 0207 935 4665 • Fax: 0207 563 4949
Green Garden House, 15-22 St Christopher's Place, London W1U 1NL
www.leeandthompson.com

## Magrath & Co
Tel: 0207 495 3003 • Fax: 0207 409 1745
52-54 Maddox Street, London W1S 1PA
www.magrath.co.uk

## P Russell & Co
Tel: 0208 742 8132 • Fax: 0208 742 8236
Gable House, 18-24 Turnham Green Terrace, London W4 1QP
e-mail: prcsolicitors@msn.com

## Russells
Tel: 0207 439 8692 • Fax: 0207 494 3582
Regency House, 1-4 Warwick Street, London W1R 6LJ
e-mail: media@russells.co.uk

## Schillings
Tel: 0207 453 2500 • Fax: 0207 453 2600
Royalty House, 72-74 Dean Street, London W1D 3TL
www.schillings.co.uk

## Seddons
Tel: 0207 725 8000 • Fax: 0207 935 5049
5 Portman Square, London W1H 6NT
www.seddons.co.uk

## Sheridans
Tel: 0207 404 0444 • Fax: 0207 831 1982
14 Red Lion Square, London WC1R 4QL
e-mail: entertainment@sheridans.co.uk

## The Simkins Partnership
Tel: 0207 907 3000 • Fax: 0207 907 3111
45-51 Whitfield Street, London W1T 4HB
www.simkins.com

## Spraggon Stennett Brabyn
Tel: 0207 938 2223 • Fax: 0207 938 2224
Crown House, 225 Kensington High Street, London W8 6SD
www.ssb.co.uk

## Statham Gill Davies

Tel: 0207 317 3210 • Fax: 0207 487 5925
52 Welbeck Street, London W1G 9XP
www.tenongroup.com

## WGS Solicitors

Tel: 0207 723 1656 • Fax: 0207 724 6936
133 Praed Street, London W2 1RN
www.wgs.co.uk

# APPENDIX 5

## Music Business Accountants

Once financial matters become a serious consideration, all artists should appoint their own independent accountant. Entertainers are the subject of specific and frequently changing tax legislation, particularly in relation to overseas touring work, and so it is best to appoint an accountant who is a specialist in the entertainment field, rather than an accountant who deals with a general range of businesses and individuals. The following list represents some of the firms which have departments specialising in the music business.

### Arram Berlyn Gardnert
Tel: 0207 400 6000 • Fax: 0207 400 6001
Holborn Hall, 100 Grays Inn Road, London WC1X 8BY
www.agggroup.co.uk

### Baker Tilly
Tel: 0207 413 5100 • Fax: 0207 413 5101
2 Bloomsbury Street, London WC1B 3ST
www.bakertilly.co.uk

### BDO Stoy Hayward
Tel: 0207 486 5888 • Fax: 0207 487 3686
8 Baker Street, London W1U 3LL
www.bdo.co.uk

### Brebner, Allen & Trapp
Tel: 0207 734 2244 • Fax: 0207 287 5315
The Quadrangle, 180 Wardour Street, London W1F 8LB
www.brebner.co.uk

### Deloitte & Touche
Tel: 0207 007 6023 • Fax: 0207 007 0177
180 The Strand, London WC2R 1BL
www.deloitte.co.uk

### Entertainment Accounting International
Tel: 0207 978 4488 • Fax: 0207 978 4492
26a Winders Road, Battersea, London SW11 3HB
e-mail: contact@eai.co.uk.com

### Ernst & Young
Tel: 0207 951 2000 • Fax: 0207 951 1345
Becket House, 1 Lambeth Palace Road, London SE1 7EU
www.ey.com

## Focus

Tel: 0207 602 6351 • Fax: 0207 300 6522
Sanctuary House, 45-53 Sinclair Road, London W14 0NS
www.sanctuarygroup.com

## Gelfand Rennert Feldman & Brown

Tel: 0207 636 1776 • Fax: 0207 636 6331
Langham House, 1b Portland Place, London W1B 1GR
e-mail: info@grfb-uk.com

## OJ Kilkenny & Company

Tel: 0207 792 9494 • Fax: 0207 792 1722
6 Landsdowne Mews, London W11 3BH
e-mail: dmoss@ojkilkenny.co.uk

## KPMG LLP

Tel: 01727 733 063 • Fax: 01727 733 001
Aquis Court, 31 Fishpool Street, St Albans AL3 4RF
www.kpmg.com

## Lubbock Fine

Tel: 0207 490 7766 • Fax: 0207 490 5102
Russell Bedford House, City Forum, 250 City Road, London EC1V 2QQ
www.lubbockfine.co.uk

## Martin Greene Ravden

Tel: 0207 625 4545 • Fax: 0207 625 5265
55 Loudoun Road, London NW8 0DL
www.mgr.co.uk

## Prager And Fenton

Tel: 0207 831 4200 • Fax: 0207 831 5080
Midway House, 27-29 Cursitor Street, London EC4A 1LT
www.pragerfenton.com

## PricewaterhouseCoopers

Tel: 0207 583 5000 • Fax: 0207 822 4652
1 Embankment Place, London WC2N 6RH
www.pwcglobal.co.uk

## Saffery Champness

Tel: 0207 841 4000 • Fax: 0207 841 4100
Lion House, Red Lion Street, London WC1R 4GB
www.saffery.com

## Sedley Richard Laurence Voulters

Tel: 0207 287 9595 • Fax: 0207 287 9696
Kendal House, 1 Conduit Street, London W1S 2XA
www.srlv.co.uk

## Sloane & Co

Tel: 0207 221 3292 • Fax: 0207 229 4810
36-38 Westbourne Grove, Newton Road, London W2 5SH
www.sloane.co.uk

# APPENDIX 6

## Sample Management Agreement

There is no such thing as a 'standard' management agreement. The example below is angled more towards the manager's interests than the artist's, and it is usually the case that the first version of any management agreement will be supplied by the manager or his solicitor to the artist.

Remember that no artist should ever, under any circumstances, either sign or agree to sign, any management agreement without the advice of an expert music industry solicitor. If any artist thinks that they are saving money by not seeking professional advice, then they are making the worst possible mistake which could cost them a great deal more in the future than they are saving in legal fees.

The format below is a short form, designed to be easily understandable whilst covering all the main issues and being legally binding. There are numerous other detailed provisions which may be inserted into a long form management agreement, some of which will related very specifically to the particular artist(s) who are the subject of the agreement.

---

[ Name(s) of Artist(s) ]

[ Address(es) of Artist(s) ]

( "You", "your" and which expression shall be deemed to include any company or other entity which provides your services now or in the future )

[ Date ]

Dear [ Name(s) of Artist(s) ]

We write to confirm the terms upon which you have engaged us to act as your Managers. Until we execute a long form management agreement with you, this agreement shall be legally binding and shall serve to reflect the terms upon which we shall operate, as follows :-

### 1. The Term

> The Term of this Agreement shall be 5 ( five ) years commencing upon the date hereof [ SAVE THAT in the event that we have not secured an offer of a recording agreement or publishing agreement for you within the period expiring 1 ( one ) year from the date hereof ( "the Notice Date" ) you shall be

entitled to give us written notice that you are terminating the Term hereof. If no such written notice is received by us within 30 ( thirty ) days of the Notice Date then the Term shall continue for the full period of 5 ( five ) years ]

## 2. The Territory

The World.

## 3. Exclusivity / The Activities

We shall act as your exclusive Managers in respect of all of your activities in the entertainment industry including but not limited to activities as a musician, recording artist, performer of any kind, songwriter, lyricist, record producer, record engineer, writer and actor ( "the Activities" ). We shall be empowered to appoint a so-called booking agent on your behalf provided that such agent's commission does not exceed 10% ( ten per cent ) of your gross income without your prior written consent.

## 4. Our Responsibilities

During the Term we shall perform all the services expected of a first class management company and shall use our best commercial endeavours to advance and promote your career in the entertainment industry in full consultation with you. We shall negotiate and ( after consulting fully with you ) execute all agreements with third parties on your behalf, acting in good faith, and shall regularly keep you advised of all matters pertaining to your career. We shall provide the services of [ Name Of "Key Person" ] to personally supervise your career, together with their support staff, and if such person is not available for a period of 45 ( forty-five ) consecutive days you may require us in writing to supply another person in their place. If such other person is not acceptable to you, acting reasonably, then you may upon 30 ( thirty ) days written notice terminate the Term.

## 5. Your Responsibilities And Warranties

By signing this agreement you warrant that you are entitled to agree to the terms hereof and that you have not made any other arrangements which will interfere with our engagement, so that we are your sole exclusive Managers in the Territory during the Term. You agree that you will not execute any agreement or make any arrangement relating to the Activities without our prior written consent, and will refer any enquiries relating to your career to us. You agree that you have taken expert independent legal advice before signing this agreement.

## 6. Our Commission Rates

You agree to pay us the following levels of Commission. Commission is payable in respect of all gross income paid or credited on your behalf either directly to you or to our client account in respect of Activities carried out during the Term. [VAT is charged on Commission ]

*Income Derived From Live Engagements:*

The greater of 15% fifteen per cent ( fifteen per cent ) of gross income or 20% ( twenty per cent ) of the Net Income. "Net Income" is defined as gross income derived from live engagements less any and all legitimate and reasonable costs incurred by you and agreed by us in writing. In respect of live engagements ( including but not limited to theatrical engagements ) in respect of which you are not required to incur any costs, Commission is payable at 20% ( twenty per cent ) of gross income.

*All Other Income:*

20% of your gross income.

We shall not charge Commission on the following areas of income :-

i)      Recording costs. In the case of so-called "recording fund" recording agreements, the actual costs up to a maximum of 50% (fifty per cent) of any overall recording fund shall be deemed to be recording costs and thus non-commissionable.

ii)     The production costs of promotional and long form videos ;

iii)    Tour support and per diems paid by a record company ;

iv)     VAT and similar taxes ;

v)      Bad debts.

# 7. The Commission Term

You agree to pay to us Commission in respect of all Activities either undertaken by you or arranged by us during the Term, whether or not completed during the Term, in perpetuity. In respect of recording agreements and publishing agreements executed prior to or during the Term, we shall only be entitled to receive Commission on recordings and compositions created under such agreements if they are created during the Term.

Commission shall be payable as income arises to you and invoiced by us accordingly [ together with VAT ]. You agree to pay us the Commission within 14 ( fourteen ) days of the receipt by you of the gross income to which such Commission relates. In the event that commissions are properly due to any prior manager in respect of Activities carried out either prior to or during the Term then such commissions shall be deductible from the Commission.

In respect of Activities carried out prior to the Term only ( "Pre-Term Activities ), we shall be entitled to commission such Pre-Term Activities at the rate of 10 % ( ten per cent ) of your gross income PROVIDED THAT such commission rate shall be reduced pro-rata by any commission liability to a prior manager, so that your aggregate commission liability never exceeds 20% ( twenty per cent ) of your gross income.

## 8. Artist Expenses

We shall be responsible for our own office costs. You will refund expenses incurred by us which are necessarily and properly incurred during the course of our activities as your Manager, including travel costs which in the case of long haul travel shall be business class, and international telephone and fax costs, and mobile telephone costs ( "Artist Expenses" ). If Artist Expenses are incurred on behalf of other artists managed by us you will only be required to refund such proportion thereof that directly relates to you. We shall be permitted to incur expenses of up to £1000 per month in aggregate without your prior consent, but we will request your consent in respect of individual expenses in excess of £300.

## 9. Indemnity

Each party hereto fully indemnifies the other against any claim, loss or damage arising out of any breach of the terms hereof.

## 10. Miscellaneous

(i) Nothing in this agreement shall be construed so as to create a partnership or joint venture between us ; (ii) We shall at all times be free to offer our managements services to other artists ; (iii) If any part of this agreement is for any reason found to be illegal or unenforceable the validity of the remainder of this agreement shall be unaffected ; (iv) The commercial terms of this agreement are confidential and shall not be disclosed to any third party ; (v) Any notices issues hereunder shall be in writing ; (vi) This agreement shall be construed according to the laws of England; (vii) Both parties hereto undertake to negotiate a long form agreement reflecting the terms hereof in good faith and execute the same as soon as practicable following the signature hereof ; (viii) We may assign the benefit of this agreement provided that we remain primarily liable for fulfilling our obligations hereunder ; (ix) [We will make available the sum of £ xxx ( xxx hundred pounds ) plus VAT as a contribution to your legal expenses in respect of this Agreement, and such sum shall be recoverable by us from you as an Artist Expense at a time to be agreed between us in good faith.]

Would you kindly indicate your agreement with the foregoing by signing and returning the attached copy hereof to us.

Yours faithfully.

## [Manager]

[ Signature ]

Read & Agreed...............................................Date...............................

## [Artist's Name]

# APPENDIX 7

## Useful Contacts

### The Fly Magazine
Tel: 0207 691 4555 • Fax: 0207 691 4666
109x Regents Park Road, London NW1 8UR
www.channelfly.com

### Hit Sheet Magazine
Tel: 0208 360 4088 • Fax: 0208 360 4088
31 the Birches, London N21 1NJ
www.hitsheet.co.uk

### Hot Press Magazine
Tel: 00 353 1 241 1500 • Fax: 00 353 1 679 5097
13 Trinity Street, Dublin 2, Ireland
www.hotpress.com

### Kerrang!
Tel: 0207 436 1515 • Fax: 0207 312 8910
EMAP Metro, Mappin House, 4 Winsley Street, London W1R 7AR
www.kerrang.com

### Logo Magazine
Mede House, Salisbury Street, Southampton S015 2TZ
www.logo-magazine.com

### Metal Hammer
Tel: 0207 317 2688
Future Publishing, 99 Baker Street, London W1U 6FP
Fax: 0207 486 5678
www.metalhammer.co.uk

### Mojo
Tel: 0207 436 1515 • Fax: 0207 312 8296
EMAP Metro, 5th Floor, Mappin House, 4 Winsley Street, London W1W 8HF
www.mojo4music.com

### Music Week
Tel: 01732 364 422 • Fax: 0207 921 8326
CMP Information, Ludgate House, 245 Ludgate House, 245 Blackfriars Road, London
SE1 9UR
www.musicweek.com

## New Musical Express
Tel: 0207 261 6472 • Fax: 0207 261 5185
IPC Magazines, Kings Reach Tower, Stamford Street, London SE1 9LS
www.nme.com

## Q
Tel: 0207 312 8182 • Fax: 0207 312 8247
EMAP Metro, Mappin House, 4 Winsley Street, London W1N 7AR
www.qonline.co.uk

## Rip & Burn Magazine
Tel: 0208 267 5186 • Fax: 0208 267 5815
38-42 Hampton Road, Teddington, Middlesex TW11 0JE
www.ripandburnmag.com

## Time Out
Tel: 0207 813 3000 • Fax: 0207 813 6158
Universal House, 251 Tottenham Court Road, London W1T 7AB
www.timeout.com

## Uncut Magazine
Tel: 0207 261 6992
IPC Music Magazines, Kings Reach Tower, Stamford Street, London SE1 9LS

# APPENDIX 8

## Sample Live Performance Agreement

Below you will find a very straightforward and brief agreement which you could send to a promoter to cover the main terms of an appearance by your band at his gig.

---

**THIS AGREEMENT** is made the (day) day of (month) (year) **BETWEEN** (name of band) of (address of band) hereinafter referred to as "the Artist" and (name of promoter) of (address of promoter) hereinafter referred to as "the Promoter".

The Artist and the Promoter hereby agree as follows:

1. The Artist shall appear at the Venue upon the Date in order to perform live in Concert for the duration specified in the definition of "the Set" herein and in consideration of such appearance by the Artist the Promoter shall pay to the Artist the Fee as set out herein.

2. The Promoter shall be entitled to sell tickets in respect of the above performance at the price specified herein, and shall provide PA and lighting equipment for use by the Artist during the performance and the Rider as specified below at no cost to the Artist.

3. Definitions

"The Venue"
shall mean The XYZ Club, Toilet Street, Dumpsville.

"The Date"
shall mean 23 August 2004.

"The Set"
shall mean 1 x performance of 60 minutes duration commencing at approximately 9pm.

"The Fee"
shall mean a guarantee of £200 payable in cash to the Artist following the completion of the performance, plus 75% of all net receipts received by the Promoter in excess of £500.

"Tickets"
shall mean tickets to the performance at £5 in advance and £6 on the door.

"PA"
shall mean a first class PA system of minimum 3K with minimum fourway monitor mix, all necessary microphones and outboard effects specified to the Promoter by the Artist's

sound engineer, and the services of a monitor engineer.

"Lights"

shall mean a first class lighting system suitable for the Venue and the services of an experienced lighting operator.

"Rider"
shall mean a full hot meal for 6 people to be provided after soundcheck, and 24 cans of good quality lager to be placed in the Artist's dressing room upon arrival at the Venue.

4.

(i) The Artist shall be given 100% top billing on all advertising and shall be entitled to select any support bands;

(ii) The Artist shall be permitted access to the venue from....... on the day of the Performance and the Promoter shall provide at no cost to the Artist the services of....... local crew to assist with the Artist's equipment;

(iii) The Promoter shall provide the Artist with a clean lockable dressing room for the Artist's exclusive use.

Read and agreed

Signed.................................................................Date........................ ...

**[The Artist]**

Signed.................................................................Date........................ ...

**[The Promoter]**

# APPENDIX 9

## London Club Venues

Many of London's best-known cub venues are listed below and there are dozens of others to be found in the pages of Time Out and the NME.

### 93 Feet East
Tel: 020 7247 3293
150 Brick Lane, London E1

### Barfly Club
Tel: 0207 691 4244 • Fax: 0207 691 4246
The Monarch, 49 Chalk Farm Road, London NW1 8AN
www.barflyclub.com

### Betsy Trotwood
Tel :020 7253 4285
55 Farringdon Road, London EC1
www.plumpromotions.co.uk

### The Borderline
Tel: 0207 395 0799 • Fax: 0207 395 0766
Orange Yard, Manette Street, Charing Cross Road, London W1V 5LB
www.borderline.co.uk

### Bull & Gate
Tel: 0207 485 5358 • Fax: 0208 806 8093
389 Kentish Town Road, London NW5 2TJ
www.bullandgate.co.uk

### Camden Underworld
Tel : 020 7482 1932
174 Camden High Street, London NW1

### Dublin Castle
Tel: 0208 806 2668 • Fax: 0208 806 6444
94 Parkway, London NW1
www.bugbearbookings.com

### Electric Ballroom
Tel: 0207 485 9006 • Fax: 0207 284 0745
184 Camden High Street, London NW1 8QP
www.electricballroom.co.uk

### Garage / Upstairs At The Garage
Tel: 0208 961 5490 or 0207 607 1818
20-22 Highbury Corner, London N5 1RD
www.meanfiddler.com

## Half Moon
Tel: 0208 780 9383
93 Lower Richmond Road, London SW15 1E U
www.halfmoon.co.uk

## Jazz Cafe
Tel: 0207 916 6060
5 Parkway, London NW1 7PG
www.jazzcafe.co.uk

## The Marquee Club
Tel: 020 7734 8690
1 Leicester Square, London WC2
www.plumpromotions.co.uk

## Mean Fiddler
Tel: 0207 434 9592
165 Charing Cross Road, London WC2H OEN
www.meanfiddler.com

## Metro Club
Tel: 0207 437 0964
19-23 Oxford Street, London
www.blowupmetro.com

## 100 Club
Tel: 0207 636 0933
100 Oxford Street, London W1D 1LL
www.100club.co.uk

## Rock Garden
Tel: 0207 257 8609
6-7 The Piazza, Covent Garden, London WC2E 8HA
www.rockgarden.co.uk

## The Spitz
Tel: 0207 392 9032
109 Commercial Street, Old Spitalfields Market, London E1 6BG
www.spitz.co.uk

## Subterania
Tel: 0208 961 4590
12 Acklam Road, London W10 5QZ

## Water Rats Theatre
Tel: 0207 837 7269
328 Grays Inn Road, London WC1X 8BZ
www.plumpromotions.co.uk

# APPENDIX 10

## Booking Agents And Promoters

### AGENTS

### The Agency Group
Tel: 0207 278 3331 • Fax: 0207 837 4672
370 City Road, London EC1V 2QA
www.theagencygroup.com

### Asgard
Tel: 0207 387 5090 • Fax: 0207 387 8740
125 Parkway, London NW1 7PS
e-mail: info@asgard-uk.com

### Coda Agency
Tel: 0207 012 1400 • Fax: 0207 012 1566
2nd Floor, 81 Rivington Street, London EC2A 3AY
www.codaagency.com

### Concorde International Artists
Tel: 0207 602 8822 • Fax: 0207 603 2352
101 Shepherds Bush Road, London W6 7LP
e-mail: cia@cia.uk.com

### Helter Skelter
Tel: 0207 376 8501 • Fax: 0207 376 8336
The Plaza, 535 Kings Road, London SW10 0SZ
e-mail: info@helterskelter.co.uk

### ITB (International Talent Booking)
Tel: 0207 379 1313 • Fax: 0207 379 1744
Ariel House, 74a Charlotte Street, London W1T 4QH
www.itb.co.uk

### Primary Talent International
Tel: 0207 833 8993 • Fax: 0207 405 4002
2 –12 Pentonville Road, London N1 9PL
www.primary.uk.com

### Solo
Tel: 0207 009 3361 • Fax: 0870 749 3174
1st Floor, Regent Arcade House, 252-260 Regents Street, London W1B 3BX
www.solo.uk.com

## VAT Agency
Tel: 0207 704 9720 • Fax: 0207 226 6135
1-2 Purley Place, London N1 1QA
www.vathq.co.uk

## PROMOTERS

### Asgard
see above

### Clear Channel
Tel: 0207 009 3333 • Fax: 0870 749 3191
1st Floor, Regent Arcade House 252–260 Regent Street, London W1B 3BX
www.clearchannel.co.uk

### Concorde
see above

### Kennedy Street Enterprises
Tel: 0161 941 5151 • Fax: 0161 928 9491
Kennedy House, 31 Stamford Street, Altrincham, Cheshire WA14 1ES
e-mail: kse@kennedystreet.com

### Marshall Arts
Tel: 0207 586 3831 • Fax: 0207 586 1422
Leeder House, 6 Erskine Road, London NW3 3AJ
www.marshall-arts.co.uk

### Phil McIntyre Promotions
Tel: 0207 439 2270 • Fax: 0207 439 2280
2nd Floor, 35 Soho Square, London W1D 3QX
e-mail: reception@pmcintyre.co.uk

### Metropolis Music
Tel: 0207 424 6800 • Fax: 0207 424 6849
69 Caversham Road, London NW5 2DR
www.gigsandtours.com

### Riverman Concerts
Tel: 0207 381 4000 • Fax: 0207 381 9666
Top Floor, George House, Brecon Road, London W6 8PY
www.riverman.co.uk

### SJM Concerts
Tel: 0161 907 3443 • Fax: 0161 907 3446
St Matthews, Liverpool Road, Manchester M3 4NQ

# APPENDIX 11

## SAMPLE LICENSE AGREEMENT

This sample is provided to illustrate the main terms of a fairly standard license agreement, in this case for an album. The key points commercial points are the Term, the Territory, the Advance and the Royalty.

Any license deal for recordings which you own should always be negotiated on your behalf by an expert music industry solicitor.

**THIS AGREEMENT** is made this      day of          200 [  ]

**BETWEEN** [ INSERT NAME OF LICENSOR ] of [ address ] (hereinafter called "the Licensor" which expression shall include its successors and assignors) of the one part and [ NAME OF RECORD COMPANY RELEASING THE RECORD ] of [ address ] (hereinafter called "the Licensee") of the other part.

**NOW IT IS HEREBY AGREED as follows:**

1. **DEFINITIONS**

   For the purposes of this Agreement, the following expressions shall have the following meanings:

(a)     "the Recordings" shall mean the sound recordings embodied on the Album entitled "[name of album]" ("the Album") comprising the following tracks:-

                    [ List Of Tracks ] ("the Recordings")

(b)     "the Artist" shall mean  [ Name Of Artist ]

(c)     "the Term" shall mean a period of  [        ] years commencing on the [ date ] and expiring on [ date ]       ("the Expiry Date").

(d)     "the Territory" shall mean [             ]

(e)     "the Royalty Rate" shall mean [ insert royalty rate(s) as appropriate together with any uplifts, deductions etc ]

(f)     "Royalty Base Price" shall mean the retail price of Records sold hereunder the Licensee's published price to dealers in respect of Records sold hereunder (delete as appropriate) (exclusive of any applicable taxes)

[ and then less the Packaging Deductions – NB only if you are prepared to agree to packaging deductions ].

(g)    "Advance" shall mean the advance set out in clause 9 hereof being a non returnable advance recoupable from royalties accruing to the Licensor hereunder.

(h)    [ "Packaging Deductions" shall mean – NB only if agreed ]

## MANUFACTURING AND SELLING RIGHTS

The Licensor grants by way of licence to the Licensee the exclusive right to manufacture and have manufactured and to sell in the Territory only during the Term records (in the form of compact discs and [ insert any other format rights granted ] ) reproducing the Recordings [ at full price ] on Licensee's top line label ("Records").

## 3.    MASTERS AND MANUFACTURING PARTS

3.1    The Licensor shall supply to the Licensee such parts as the Licensee shall require for the purpose of manufacturing Records for which the Licensee shall pay to the Licensor on demand the full manufacturing costs of such parts together with all shipping costs in connection therewith.

3.2    The Licensee shall not use the said parts not permit the use thereof for any purpose other than the manufacture of Records as provided for in this Agreement.

3.3    The copyright and the property in the Recordings shall remain vested in the Licensor, but all copies and derivatives of such Recordings made by or for the Licensee shall be and remain the property of the Licensee subject to the provisions of clause 13 hereof.

3.3.1    The Licensor shall supply to the Licensee at the Licensee's expense copy artwork for the purpose of the packaging of Records derived from the Recordings. [ The Licensor shall as far as it is practical to do so ensure that all its other Licensees use identical artwork with territorial variations as required and the Licensee shall be entitled to incorporate the Licensee's logo in addition to the Licensor's logo ]

3.3.2    The Licensee shall consult with the Licensor in respect of artwork and packaging generally.

3.3.3    The Licensee shall make a non-recoupable contribution of £ [    ] towards the Licensor's artwork origination costs.

[ 3.4    The Licensor shall supply to the Licensee promotional video footage of the titles "                            " and "                        " which exists at the date of this Agreement and such footage shall be made available to the Licensee on payment of shipping costs and copy master costs and the non-recoupable sum of                          per title upon delivery thereof. ]

## 4. ARTISTS NAMES AND PHOTOGRAPHS

4.1    The Licensee shall have the right and license at all times during the Term hereof to use and publish the names and approved photographs of the Artist featured on the

Recordings for the purpose of packaging, labeling, cataloguing and exploiting the Records, but the use of any such photographs except in accordance with artwork supplied by the Licensor must have the prior written approval of the Licensor.

4.2    The Licensee shall ensure that on the packaging of all Records released hereunder the credit shall be in a form approved by the Licensor PROVIDED THAT any artwork supplied by the Licensor shall be deemed to be approved.

## 5. WARRANTIES OF TITLE

The Licensor warrants:

(a)    that prior to the despatch to the Licensee of the Recordings the Licensor will have obtained all relevant consents (except those provided in clause 7 hereto) for the manufacture and sale of Records and for the use and publication by the Licensee of the names and photographs of the Artist;

(b)    that it possesses full power and authority to enter into and to perform this Agreement and that there are no liens or encumbrances against any of the Recordings which would derogate from or be inconsistent with the rights granted to the Licensee hereunder.

## 6. LICENSEE'S OBLIGATIONS

6.1.    The Licensee shall not:

(a)    release Records of the Recordings or otherwise exploit the Recordings in any form other than that of the Masters supplied hereunder;

(b)    manufacture of have manufactured Records except from Recordings supplied hereunder;

(c)    change the artwork designs as supplied by the Licensor (if any) for the Records of the Recordings except with the prior written approval of the Licensor;

(d)    sell or distribute records as premium records or at mid price or low price or budget price or as deletions or cut outs or close out sales without the Licensor's prior written consent ;

(e)    export Records from the Territory directly or indirectly or supply Records to third parties that it knows or suspects to being engaged in exporting Records from the Territory;

(f)    remix or edit in any form any of the Recordings.

6.2     The Licensee shall:

(a)     guarantee a release date for the Album in the Territory of [     ] ("the Release Date") and shall advise the Licensor within seven (7) days of the Release Date of Records released hereunder the coupling numbers of the same in the Territory;

(b)     supply to the Licensor at the Licensee's own cost ten samples of Records (in each format) after manufacture and in any event upon or as soon as possible after first release by the Licensee in the Territory;

(c)     manufacture or have manufactured Records to the highest standards available in the Territory;

(d)     procure that all Records sold hereunder bear on the labels and packaging thereof all copyright or other symbols or words necessary to protect the rights of the Licensor and a logo credit is given on sleeves and pressings in a form to be provided by the Licensor and that there is a credit in favour of the Licensor in the following form:

"Under license from                                         , London"

## 7.     MECHANICAL COPYRIGHT

The Licensee shall be solely responsible for the fulfilment of all mechanical copyright obligations arising out of the manufacture and sale of Records hereunder. Further the Licensee shall fully indemnify the Licensor from and against the consequences of any breach of this obligation including all costs or damages (including legal fees) incurred or suffered by the Licensor arising out of the failure to comply with the requirements so laid down.

## 8.     ROYALTY PROVISIONS

8.1     The Licensee shall pay to the Licensor a royalty in respect of one hundred per cent (100%) of Records sold and not returned.  Such royalty shall be at the Royalty Rate calculated on the Royalty Base Price.

8.2     The Licensee shall pay to the Licensor [ insert percentage ] of all fees, income or other monies received from third parties by the Licensee in respect of the use or exploitation of the Recordings PROVIDED THAT in all such cases the Licensee shall have obtained the prior written approval of the Licensor in respect of such third party exploitation.

8.3     The Licensee shall furnish to the Licensor within sixty (60) days of 31st March, 30th June, 30th September and 31st December in each year a statement showing the number of Records sold since the date of the previous statement and any other exploitation in respect thereof and the amount of royalty due in respect of such sales and other exploitation and the Licensee shall at such time pay such amount to the Licensor.

8.4     The Licensee shall furnish to the Licensor with each statement details of [ the Retail Price/Published Price to Dealers (delete as appropriate) ] of each Record in the Territory in all formats.

8.5     The Licensor shall have the right to inspect, or appoint an accountant to inspect, the books of the Licensee and of any party manufacturing Records for the Licensee in so far as the said books relate to sales and any monies or royalties payable to the Licensor hereunder.  In the event that any such inspection reveals any statement rendered to the Licensor hereunder to be in error in favour of the Licensee the costs and expenses of such inspection shall be borne by the Licensee and the Licensee shall forthwith pay to the Licensor the amount of such under payment together with interest thereon at 2% above Barclays Bank Plc base rate as shall be applicable from time to time in addition to any other rights and remedies the Licensor may have in respect thereof. Prompt and correct rendering of statements and payment of royalties by the Licensee to the Licensor shall be of the essence of this Agreement.

8.6     For the purposes of calculating the royalties due to the Licensor hereunder any Records that are manufactured and are not reported as having been sold or destroyed shall be deemed to have been sold at full price.

## 9.     ADVANCES

The Licensee shall pay to the Licensor the sum of  £ [          ] payable [ 50% (fifty per cent) ] upon signature hereof and the balance upon delivery of the Album [ insert details of how Advance is to be paid, for example by telegraphic transfer ]

## 10.     ASSIGNMENT

The Licensee shall not transfer or assign this Agreement or any rights acquired hereunder to any person, firm or corporation without the prior written consent of the Licensor except that the Licensee may have Records manufactured by a third party in the Territory.

## 11.     BROADCAST INCOME

Licensor reserves all public performance and broadcasting rights in respect of all copies of the Recording hereunder and the Licensee undertakes to notify any such relevant Collecting Society in the Territory ("CS") of Licensor's rights as aforesaid together with such copyright information as may require.  Licensee shall send Licensor a copy of such notice.  In the event that CS makes any payment to the Licensee in respect of any of the Recordings hereunder the Licensee undertakes to pay such monies to Licensor in the next accounting period.

## 12.     LICENSOR'S RIGHT OF TERMINATION

The Licensor shall have the right to immediately terminate this Agreement without notice in the event of:

(a)     the liquidation or bankruptcy of the Licensee either voluntary or compulsory, but this shall not include a voluntary liquidation for the purposes of reconstruction;

(b)     the appointment of a Receiver liquidator manager or trustee in bankruptcy of the Licensee;

(c)      the acquisition of a majority interest in the Licensee's business by any other person, firm, Licensor or Government authority;

(d)      a breach by the Licensee of any of the conditions of this Agreement which breach shall not have been remedied within thirty (30) days of notice being given by the

Licensor to the Licensee to remedy such breach.

## 13.    TERMINATION PROVISIONS

Upon the Expiry Date and without prejudice to any accrued rights or claims which the Licensor may have against the Licensee:

(a)      the Licensee shall cease to use or permit to be used for the manufacture of Records the Recordings supplied hereunder and all derivatives and copies thereof and shall notify the Licensor of the same.  The Licensee shall at the written option of the Licensor either destroy or erase such Recordings and derivatives and copies and the Licensee shall furnish a sworn statement of that fact by a principal officer of the Licensee;

(b)      the Licensee shall supply to the Licensor within twenty one (21) days of the Expiry Date a written inventory of existing stocks and then except where this Agreement is terminated pursuant to clause 12 hereof  the Licensee shall be entitled on a non exclusive basis to sell off such stocks for a period of six (6) months from the Expiry Date and shall continue to account to the Licensor for royalties as provided for in this Agreement PROVIDED THAT during the last 6 (six) months of the Term the Licensee shall not manufacture more Records than have been manufactured during the preceding nine (9) months.  At the expiry of such six (6) month period the Licensee shall at the written option of the Licensor either destroy the remaining Records which are still in its possession or under its control or sell the same to the Licensor at the full manufacturing cost thereof and the Licensee shall also if requested by the Licensor and in the event that the Licensor has exercised its option of requiring destruction furnish a sworn statement of that fact by a principal officer of the Licensee;

(c)      Upon termination of this Agreement (whether by effluxion of time or otherwise howsoever and pursuant to any clause herein) the Licensee shall have no right to claim from the Licensor damages or compensation (howsoever caused) alleged by the Licensee to arise out of the termination of this Agreement and by its signature hereto the Licensee expressly waives any such right or claim.

## 14.    DEFAULT

14.1    The Licensee agrees to fully indemnify the Licensor and undertakes to hold it harmless from any and all losses, damages, costs and expenses (including, but not limited to reasonable legal fees) arising out of:

(a)      any breach by the Licensee of the representations and undertakings made by it herein; and/or;

(b)      any use by the Licensee of the Recordings in a manner not authorised under the Agreement.

14.2    The Licensor agrees to fully indemnify the Licensee and undertakes to hold it harmless from any and all losses, costs and expenses (including, but not limited to reasonable legal fees) arising out of any breach by the Licensor of the Licensor's warranties representations and undertakings made by it herein.

## 15    FORCE MAJEURE

Neither the Licensor nor the Licensee shall be deemed in default of this Agreement if the performance of any of their respective obligations hereunder is delayed or becomes impossible of performance for any reason beyond its reasonable control. The Licensor shall be entitled to treat this Agreement as non exclusive for the duration of such event and to the extent that the Agreement cannot be enforced or performed according to its terms for a period in excess of six (6) months then this Agreement shall be deemed to have terminated at the end of such six months period.

## 16.    MISCELLANEOUS

16.1    Nothing in this Agreement shall be construed as being a partnership between the parties and no variation of this Agreement shall be binding unless made in writing and signed by the person duly authorised to make such variation on the part of the Licensor.

16.2    The clause headings in this Agreement are for information only and do not form part of this Agreement.

16.3.1    Any notice required to be given in pursuance of this Agreement shall be in writing and be delivered by hand or sent to the address of the party to be served at the address mentioned in this Agreement or to the last known address of that party such change of address to be made in accordance with the provisions of this clause and any notice given to the Licensor shall be marked for the attention of [                    ]

16.3.2    All notices shall be sent by facsimile (transmission confirmation report required) and a copy sent by first class prepaid or recorded delivery letter within the United Kingdom and by prepaid or certified airmail letter outside the United Kingdom and five (5) days after the date of mailing of any such notice (or one day in respect of a facsimile transmission) shall be deemed the date of the receipt thereof. Such facsimile transmission shall be sent to Licensee' facsimile number: [                    ]
and to Licensor's facsimile number: +or such other number as Licensee or Licensor shall so advise the other in writing.

16.4    If any part of this Agreement is determined to be void, invalid, inoperative or unenforceable by a Court of competent jurisdiction or by any other legally constituted body having jurisdiction to make such determination the remainder of this Agreement shall continue with full force and effect.

16.5    This Agreement shall be governed by the laws of England and the High Court of Justice in London shall be the exclusive Court of Jurisdiction.

AS WITNESS the hands of the parties hereto the day and year first before written

Signed _____
For and on behalf of [ The Licensor ]

Signed _____
For and on behalf of [ The Licensee ]

# APPENDIX 12

## London Rehearsal Rooms

### Backstreet Rehearsal Studios
Tel: 0207 609 1313 • Fax: 0207 609 5229
313 Holloway Road, Islington, London N7 9SU
www.backstreet.co.uk

### Bush Studios
Tel: 0208 740 1740 • Fax: 0208 740 1740
The Arches, 152 Macfarlane Road, London W12 7LA
www.bushstudios.co.uk

### John Henry's Limited
Tel: 0207 609 9181 • Fax: 0207 700 7040
16-24 Brewery Road, London N7 9NH
www.johnhenrys.com

### The Joint
Tel: 0207 833 3375 • Fax: 0207 833 1178
1-6 Field Street, London WC1X 9DG
www.thejoint.org.uk

### The Premises Studios Limited
Tel: 0207 729 7593 • Fax: 0207 739 5600
201-205 Hackney Road, London E2 8JL
www.premises.demon.co.uk

### Ritz Rehearsals Studios
Tel: 0208 870 1335 • Fax: 0208 877 1036
110-112 Disraeli Road, Putney, London SW15 2DX

### Terminal Studios
Tel: 0207 403 3050 • Fax: 0207 407 6123
4-10 Lamb Walk, London Bridge, London SE1 3TT
www.terminal.co.uk

### Waterloo Sunset
Tel: 0207 252 0001 • Fax: 0207 231 3002
Top Floor, Building D, Tower Bridge Business Complex, 100 Clements Road, London
SE16 4DG
www.musicbank.org

# APPENDIX 13

## Distributors

An exhaustive list of distributors would contain hundreds of names, but those listed below are a mixture of major names, independents and specialists.

### Absolute Marketing and Distribution
Tel: 0208 540 4242 • Fax: 0208 540 6056
The Old Lamp Works, Rodney Place, Wimbledon, London SW19 2LQ
www.absolutemarketing.co.uk

### Amato
Tel: 0208 838 8330 • Fax:0208 838 8331
58-60 Minerva Road, London NW10 6HJ
www.amatodistribution.co.uk

### Backs
Tel: 01603 624 290 • Fax: 01603 619 999
St Mary's Works, St Mary's Plain, Norwich, Norfolk NR3 3AF
info@backsrecords.co.uk

### Cadiz Music Limited
Tel: 0208 692 4691 • Fax: 0208 469 3300
2 Greenwich Quay, Clarence Road, London SE8 3EY

### Cargo Records UK Limited
Tel: 0207 731 5125
17 Heathmans Road, Parsons Green, London SW6 4TJ
www.cargorecords.co.uk

### EMI Distribution
Tel: 01926 466 300 • Fax: 01926 466 392
Hermes Close, Tachbrook Park, Leamington Spa CV34 6RP

### Essential UK Direct
Tel: 0208 833 2888 • Fax: 0208 833 2967
Auriol Drive, Greenford Park, Greendford, Middlesex UB6 0DS
www.entuk.co.uk

### Fierce! Distribution
Tel: 01243 558 444 • Fax: 01243 558 455
PO Box Arundel, West Sussex BN18 0UQ
www.fiercedistribution.com

## Golds

Tel: 0208 501 9600 • Fax: 0208 527 3604

Uplands Business Park, Blackhorse Lane, Walthamstow, London E17 5QJ

www.sgolds.co.uk

## Lightning Export

Tel: 0208 920 1250 • Fax: 0208 920 1252

141 High Street, Southgate, London N14 6BX

www.the.co.uk

## Nova Sales & Distribution (UK) Limited

Tel: 0208 390 3322 • Fax: 0208 390 3338

Isabel House, 46 Victoria Road, Surbiton, Surrey KT6 4JL

www.novadist.co.uk

## Pinnacle Records

Tel: 01689 870 622 • Fax: 01689 899 098

Osprey House, New Mill Road, Orpington, Kent BR5 3QJ

www.pinnacle-entertainment.co.uk

## Plastic Head Music Distribution Limited

Tel: 01491 825 029 • Fax: 01491 826 320

Avtech House, Hithercroft, Wallingford, Oxfordshire OX10 9DA

www.plastichead.com

## Proper Music Distribution

Tel: 0870 444 0800 • Fax: 0870 444 0801

The Powerhouse, Cricket Lane, Beckenham, Kent BR3 1LW

## Shellshock Distribution

Tel: 0208 800 8110 • Fax: 0208 800 8140

23A Collingwood Road, London N15 4LD

www.shellshock.co.uk

## SRD (Southern Records Distribution)

Tel: 0208 802 3000 • Fax: 0208 802 4444

70 Lawrence Road, London N15 4EG

www.southern.com

## Ten (The Entertainment Network)

Tel: 01296 426 151 • Fax: 01296 481 009

Rabans Lane, Aylesbury, Bucks HP19 7TS

www.ten-net.com

## Unique Distribution

Tel: 01204 675 500 • Fax: 01204 479 005

Unit 12, Lodge Bank, Industrial Estate, Off Crown Lane, Horwich, Bolton BL6 5HY

www.uniquedist.co.uk

## Vital Distribution
Tel: 0208 324 2400 • Fax: 0208 324 0001
338A Ladbroke Grove, London W10 5AH
www.vitaluk.com

# Manufacturers

## 10th Planet
Tel: 0207 637 9500 • Fax: 0207 637 9599
42-44 Newman Street, London W1P 3PA
www.10thplanet.net

## A2Z Music Services
Tel: 0207 284 8800 • Fax: 0207 284 8811
C/o Key Production, 8 Jeffrey's Place, London NW1 9PP
www.keyproduction.co.uk

## Cops
Tel: 0208 778 8556 • Fax: 0208 676 9716
The Studio, Kent House Station Approach, Barnmead Road, Beckenham, Kent BR3 1JD
www.cops.co.uk

## Hiltongrove Multimedia
Tel: 0208 521 2424 • Fax: 0208 521 4343
The Hiltongrove Business Centre, Hatherley Mews, Walthamstow, London E17 4QP
www.hiltongrove.com

## Key Production
Tel: 0207 284 8800 • Fax: 0207 284 8811
C/o Key Production, 8 Jeffrey's Place, London NW1 9PP
www.keyproduction.co.uk

## Music Media Manufacturers
Tel: 0208 265 6364 • Fax: 0208 265 6423
Unit 11D, Block F, Parkhall Road Trading Estate, 40 Martell Road, London SE21 8EN
www.musicmedia-uk.com

## RPM
Tel: 0208 960 7222 • Fax: 0208 968 1378
Unit 6, Grand Union Centre, West Row, London W10 5AS
www.rpmuk.com

## Sound Performance
Tel: 0208 691 2121 • Fax: 0208 691 3144
3 Greenwich Quay, Clarence Road, London SE8 3EY
www.soundperformance.co.uk